THE JOY OF LIVING AND THE JOY OF FINE FOOD
COME TOGETHER IN
CORINNE T. NETZER'S
101 LOW FAT RECIPES

YOU CAN LIVE A LONGER, HEALTHIER LIFE
BY CUTTING DOWN ON FAT—AND STILL HAVE
ALL THE PLEASURE OF FLAVORFUL, SATISFYING
MEALS LIKE THIS ONE:

The Appetizer
◆ Tiny Clams Steamed with Tomatoes

The Soup
◆ Wild Rice Bisque

The Entrée
◆ Veal Chops with Mushrooms and Sage

Side Dishes
◆ Braised Artichokes Roman Style
◆ Herb and Shallot Corn Bread

Dessert
◆ Apple Pear Shortcakes with Ginger Cream

IT'S ELEGANT, IT'S EASY—AND IT'S LOW FAT!

D1503081

101 LOW FAT RECIPES

QUANTITY SALES

Most Dell books are available at special quantity discounts when purchased in bulk by corporations, organizations, or groups. Special imprints, messages, and excerpts can be produced to meet your needs. For more information, write to: Dell Publishing, 666 Fifth Avenue, New York, NY 10103. Attention: Director, Diversified Sales.

Please specify how you intend to use the books (e.g., promotion, resale, etc.).

INDIVIDUAL SALES

Are there any Dell books you want but cannot find in your local stores? If so, you can order them directly from us. You can get any Dell book currently in print. For a complete up-to-date listing of our books and information on how to order, write to: Dell Readers Service, Box DR, 666 Fifth Avenue, New York, NY 10103.

THE

CORINNE T. NETZER

GOOD EATING SERIES

▶▶▶▶▶▶▶▶▶▶▶▶▶▶▶

101 LOW FAT
RECIPES

◆◆◆◆◆

Corinne T. Netzer

A Dell Trade Paperback

A DELL TRADE PAPERBACK

Published by
Dell Publishing
a division of
Bantam Doubleday Dell Publishing Group, Inc.
666 Fifth Avenue
New York, New York 10103

Designed by Rhea Braunstein

Illustrated by Alice Sorensen

ISBN: 0-440-50418-X

Printed in the United States of America
Published simultaneously in Canada
February 1993
10 9 8 7 6 5 4 3 2 1
HCR

CONTENTS

INTRODUCTION

101 Low Fat Recipes is one of five books that comprise my Good Eating series of cookbooks. (The other books are *101 Low Calorie Recipes, 101 Low-Cholesterol Recipes, 101 Low Sodium Recipes,* and *101 High Fiber Recipes*).

While we are all aware of the many excellent reasons to reduce our intake of fat, we are often reluctant or unable to do so because it generally means a sacrifice in flavor, or eating foods with no flavor at all.

To me, *Good Eating* means food that is flavorful as well as healthful. The recipes in this book have passed the taste test with flying colors, and, while the emphasis here is on dishes that are low in fat, attention has also been paid to the overall health values.

Here, you will find dishes to suit every palate and every occasion. And to help you keep track of your dietary fat intake, each recipe gives the total fat gram count per serving or portion. These calculations are based on the latest nutritional data obtained from the United States Department of Agriculture and from information supplied by the various food producers and processors.

Enjoy!

C.T.N.

SAUCES and DRESSINGS

◆ ◆ ◆ ◆ ◆

THICK AND RICH
TOMATO SAUCE

▶ ▶

Use this easy-to-prepare, very low fat, cholesterol free sauce over pasta and vegetables, for grilling and broiling, as a base for soups and stews—in short, whenever a full-bodied, tasty tomato sauce is required.

1	28-ounce can no-salt-added plum tomatoes, coarsely chopped, undrained
1/4	cup dry red wine
1/2	cup finely minced onions
2	tablespoons chopped fresh basil or 1 tablespoon dried
1 1/2	tablespoons chopped fresh parsley or 2 teaspoons dried
2	teaspoons chopped fresh oregano or 1 teaspoon dried
2	cloves garlic, pressed
	Salt and freshly ground pepper to taste

1. Combine all ingredients in a large saucepan and cook over high heat until mixture starts to boil. Cover, reduce heat, and simmer gently, stirring occasionally, for 30 minutes.

2. Remove cover and simmer for an additional 5 minutes.

MAKES ABOUT 3 CUPS
APPROXIMATELY .7 GRAM FAT PER CUP

◆ ◆ ◆ ◆ ◆

COOL YOGURT SAUCE

▶ ▶

This unusual sauce is ideal for dipping spicy barbecued meats or poultry.

1¹/₂   cups low fat plain yogurt
2   scallions, white and tender greens, finely minced
1   tablespoon fresh lime juice
¹/₂   cup chopped fresh cilantro
       Salt and freshly ground pepper to taste
1   teaspoon brown sugar
2   tablespoons chopped fresh mint leaves or 1
       tablespoon dried
       Dash hot pepper sauce, or to taste

Combine all ingredients and whisk until well blended. Cover and refrigerate for at least 1 hour. Whisk or stir well before serving.

MAKES ABOUT 1¹/₂ CUPS
APPROXIMATELY .2 GRAM FAT PER TABLESPOON

◆ ◆ ◆ ◆ ◆

LIGHT PESTO WITH PARSLEY

▶ ▶

This dish is traditionally made with a large quantity of olive oil, but my low fat version replaces most of the oil with chicken broth. My adaptation also includes parsley for a slightly milder taste, but feel free to substitute all basil if you prefer a more classically flavored Italian pesto.

Pesto is great not only over pasta but also stirred into soups or spread over pizza crust. A tablespoon or two added to low fat ricotta or cottage cheese makes a delicious stuffing for tomatoes.

This recipe is easily doubled or tripled and freezes well. I make it during the summer when fresh basil is plentiful and freeze it for use throughout the winter. (If you plan to freeze the sauce, do not add the cheese until the pesto has been defrosted and is ready to use.)

> 2   *tablespoons pine nuts*
> 2   *large cloves garlic, halved*
> 1   *cup tightly packed fresh parsley leaves*
> 1¹/₂   *cups tightly packed fresh basil leaves*
> 1   *tablespoon olive oil*
> ¹/₂   *cup Low Fat Chicken Broth (page 43) or canned low sodium broth*
> 2   *tablespoons freshly grated Parmesan or Romano cheese*
>   *Salt and freshly ground pepper to taste*

Combine all ingredients in a food processor. Blend with an on/off motion, scraping down sides of bowl often, for about 30 seconds or until smooth.

MAKES ABOUT 1 CUP
APPROXIMATELY 1.8 GRAMS FAT PER TABLESPOON

◆ ◆ ◆ ◆ ◆

SWEET AND TANGY
GRILLING SAUCE

► ►

This oil-free sauce can be used to grill anything from fish to vegetables. But don't limit it to the barbecue—use it as a marinade and as a broiling, roasting, and dipping sauce.

    2   cups low sodium tomato sauce
  1/2   cup cider vinegar
    3   tablespoons firmly packed brown sugar
    1   tablespoon Worcestershire or low sodium soy
        sauce
    2   cloves garlic, pressed
    2   teaspoons dry mustard
        Salt and freshly ground pepper to taste
        Pinch cayenne or dash hot pepper sauce, or to
        taste

1. Combine tomato sauce and vinegar in a saucepan. Cook over high heat until mixture starts to boil. Reduce heat to low, add sugar, and stir until dissolved.

2. Add remaining ingredients and cook over low heat, stirring often, for 5 minutes.

MAKES ABOUT 2¹/₂ CUPS
APPROXIMATELY .1 GRAM FAT PER ¹/₄ CUP

MUSHROOM AND ONION GRAVY

Well-browned onions help give this delicious gravy its rich color and taste. You'll find numerous uses for this recipe: spoon it over plain boiled or broiled chicken, meat or fish, use it to spruce up leftovers, mix it with barley or buckwheat groats for a tasty side dish, or, for those who crave mashed potatoes with gravy, add a tablespoon to my Creamy Whipped Potatoes (page 171) for a satisfying treat.

2	teaspoons vegetable oil
	Vegetable oil cooking spray
1	large onion, chopped
1	clove garlic, minced
6	ounces mushrooms, wiped clean and thinly sliced
1½	cups Low Fat Chicken Broth (page 43) or canned low-sodium broth
2	teaspoons Worcestershire sauce
1	tablespoon superfine flour
	Salt and freshly ground pepper to taste

1. Heat oil in a large nonstick skillet coated with cooking spray. Add onion and cook over medium heat, stirring often, until onion starts to brown.

2. Add garlic and continue to cook, stirring, until onion is very brown, but do not allow it to burn.

3. Stir mushrooms into skillet along with ½ cup of the broth and the Worcestershire sauce. Bring to a simmer over medium heat, stirring often, and cook for about 5 minutes or

until mushrooms have softened and most of the liquid has evaporated.

4. Stir flour into remaining cup of broth until dissolved and add to skillet. Reduce heat to low and stir until gravy thickens. Taste and add salt and pepper, if desired.

MAKES ABOUT 1¾ CUPS
APPROXIMATELY 2.3 GRAMS FAT PER ¼ CUP

◆ ◆ ◆ ◆ ◆

OIL-FREE HERB VINAIGRETTE

▶ ▶

This all-purpose dressing for mixed greens, potato, rice, or pasta salad also makes a tasty marinade.

> ³/₄   cup Low Fat Chicken Broth (page 43), or canned low-sodium broth
> ¹/₄   cup red wine vinegar
> 1   tablespoon fresh lemon juice
> 2   tablespoons water
> ¹/₂   teaspoon minced fresh parsley
> 2   tablespoons chopped chives or minced scallions
> ¹/₄   teaspoon dried tarragon
> ¹/₄   teaspoon dried rosemary
> ¹/₄   teaspoon dried thyme
>   Salt and freshly ground pepper to taste

Combine liquids in a jar with a tight-fitting lid. Add remaining ingredients and shake vigorously to blend. Refrigerate for at least 1 hour and shake well before using.

MAKES ABOUT 1¹/₄ CUPS
APPROXIMATELY .1 GRAM FAT PER TABLESPOON

◆ ◆ ◆ ◆ ◆

MUSTARD VINAIGRETTE
WITH SHERRY

▶ ▶

You can serve this dressing as is or spruce it up with freshly chopped herbs, a hint of crumbled blue cheese, or a dollop of low fat plain yogurt. It keeps well for several days in the refrigerator. Just whisk or shake it to bring it back to its creamy consistency.

> $^1/_2$ *cup Low Fat Chicken Broth (page 43) or canned low-sodium broth*
> $^1/_4$ *cup red wine vinegar*
> 2   *tablespoons water*
> 2   *teaspoons dry sherry*
> 1   *tablespoon Dijon mustard*
> 4   *teaspoons olive oil*
> 1   *teaspoon minced fresh parsley or $^1/_2$ teaspoon dried*
>   *Salt and freshly ground pepper to taste*

Combine broth, vinegar, water, sherry, and mustard and whisk vigorously. Add oil in a steady stream and continue whisking until slightly thickened. Stir in parsley and salt and pepper, if desired.

MAKES ABOUT 1 CUP
APPROXIMATELY 1.3 GRAMS FAT PER TABLESPOON

◆ ◆ ◆ ◆ ◆

CREAMY SHALLOT DRESSING

▶ ▶

I often use this to dress up tuna and shrimp salads, but it goes equally well mixed with vegetables or cold pasta.

1	cup low fat (1%) cottage cheese
1/4	cup low fat plain yogurt
1/4	cup fresh lemon juice or white wine vinegar
1/2	teaspoon dried tarragon
2	medium shallots, quartered
1/4	cup loosely packed fresh parsley
	Salt and freshly ground pepper to taste

Combine all ingredients in a blender or food processor and process until smooth. Chill for at least 1 hour to blend flavors before serving.

MAKES ABOUT 1³/₄ CUPS

APPROXIMATELY .1 GRAM FAT PER TABLESPOON

◆ ◆ ◆ ◆ ◆

TOFU GINGER DRESSING

▶ ▶

This slightly tart dressing is the perfect foil for cold, spicy chicken.

$^1/_4$ *pound soft tofu, rinsed, drained, and coarsely chopped*
$^3/_4$ *cup low fat plain yogurt*
3 *tablespoons fresh lemon juice*
1 *small clove garlic, quartered*
1 *tablespoon freshly grated ginger root*
1 *scallion, white and tender greens, minced*
  Salt and freshly ground pepper to taste

1. Combine tofu, yogurt, lemon juice, and garlic in a blender or food processor and process until smooth.

2. Transfer tofu mixture to a bowl, stir in ginger and scallion, and season to taste with salt and pepper. Chill for at least 1 hour before serving.

MAKES ABOUT 1$^1/_4$ CUPS
APPROXIMATELY .4 GRAM FAT PER TABLESPOON

◆ ◆ ◆ ◆ ◆

GOLDEN CHICK-PEA DRESSING

▶ ▶

T ry this dressing on an otherwise unadorned green salad
or in a pita stuffed with greens, cucumber, low fat cheese,
sprouts, and whatever else you fancy.

3/4 *cup chick-peas, cooked or canned, rinsed and
      drained*
1/4 *cup water*
2   *tablespoons fresh lemon juice, or more to taste*
1   *tablespoon cider vinegar*
1   *large clove garlic, quartered*
    Salt and freshly ground pepper to taste
    Paprika, mild or hot, to taste

1. Puree all ingredients, except salt and pepper and paprika, in a food processor or blender. If mixture is very thick,
add additional lemon juice or water according to your prefer-
ence.
2. Correct seasonings, if necessary, and chill for at least 1
hour. Bring to room temperature and sprinkle with paprika
before serving.

MAKES ABOUT 1 CUP
APPROXIMATELY .2 GRAM FAT PER TABLESPOON

APPETIZERS and STARTERS

♦ ♦ ♦ ♦ ♦

CHILLED FISH TERRINE

▶ ▶

Appetizers set the scene and tone of a meal, foreshadowing the style of the dishes that follow. A first course should be a light introduction to the courses to come, teasing rather than satisfying the appetite. My Chilled Fish Terrine, an elegant and refreshing treat on a hot summer's eve, has all these qualities.

Don't be put off by the number of ingredients or the steps for preparation. Once you read the recipe through and get a mental image of the dish, everything will fall into place like the stray pieces of a jigsaw puzzle. And the results will be well worth your efforts.

	Vegetable oil cooking spray
6	ounces scallops, quartered if large
8 to 10	large fresh spinach leaves, trimmed and rinsed
4	sole fillets, skinned (about 1 pound)
1	tablespoon chopped fresh parsley
	Zest of ¹/₂ medium lemon
	Salt and freshly ground pepper to taste
²/₃	cup dry white wine
1	packet unflavored gelatin
3	tablespoons dry vermouth or dry white wine
6¹/₈	ounce can water-packed light tuna, drained
¹/₂	cup cooked fresh or frozen chopped spinach, well drained
¹/₃	cup low fat plain yogurt
	Lemon slices and watercress for garnish

1. Line the bottom and sides of a 5- by 8-inch loaf pan with wax paper sprayed lightly with cooking oil and set aside.

2. In a large skillet, bring 1 cup of water to a boil, add scallops, reduce heat, and simmer gently for about 3 minutes or until scallops are tender. Drain scallops and set aside.

3. In the same skillet, blanch spinach leaves in boiling water for 30 seconds. Remove spinach and plunge into cold water to refresh. Drain well and spread out flat. Wipe skillet clean.

4. Line the bottom and sides of prepared loaf pan with 6 to 8 of the blanched spinach leaves, reserving two leaves to cover the top.

5. Sprinkle sole fillets with parsley, lemon zest, and salt and pepper. Roll up neatly and secure with toothpicks. Add ²/₃ cup wine to the skillet and bring to a boil. Reduce heat and place rolled fish in skillet, cover, and simmer gently for 5 minutes. Remove sole with a slotted spoon, carefully pull out toothpicks, and set fish rolls aside. Transfer cooking liquid to a food processor.

6. Sprinkle gelatin over the vermouth or wine in a small bowl and let stand for 1 minute. Place bowl in a pan of hot water and let stand, stirring frequently, for about 2 minutes or until gelatin has dissolved.

7. Meanwhile, add tuna, cooked spinach, yogurt, and half of the scallops to cooking liquid in the food processor and process for 10 seconds or until smooth. Transfer mixture to a bowl and stir in vermouth with gelatin and remaining scallops.

8. Spread half of the tuna mixture over bottom of the loaf pan. Lay the sole fillets on top—two by two, lengthwise and parallel to the 8-inch side of pan—pressing them gently into tuna mixture. Cover with remaining tuna mixture, top

with the reserved spinach leaves, and press gently. Cover and refrigerate for at least 4 hours or until well chilled.

9. Unmold very carefully (if necessary, place pan momentarily in hot water), cut into 12 equal slices, arrange on a serving platter and garnish with lemon and watercress, if desired.

SERVES 6
APPROXIMATELY 1.7 GRAMS FAT PER SERVING

♦ ♦ ♦ ♦

TINY CLAMS STEAMED
WITH TOMATOES

▶ ▶

I can down clams with the enthusiasm of a pelican! And I have been known to devour this starter all by myself shamelessly using just-torn pieces of crusty Italian bread to sop up every drop of the delicious sauce with the hedonistic abandon of Attila the Hungry!

1	teaspoon oil
2	cloves garlic, chopped
3	ripe medium tomatoes, peeled, seeded, and coarsely chopped, or 1¼ cups canned no-salt-added tomatoes, undrained
½	teaspoon hot red pepper flakes, or to taste
1	cup dry white wine
1	tablespoon Pernod or other anise-flavored liqueur (*optional*)
	Juice of 1 large lemon
½	teaspoon fennel seeds
1	tablespoon chopped fresh oregano or 1 teaspoon dried
2	dozen littleneck clams, scrubbed
4	large fresh basil leaves, slivered

1. Heat oil in large nonstick skillet, add garlic and sauté over medium heat until garlic barely begins to color. Raise heat, add tomatoes with any accumulated juice, and hot pepper flakes if desired, and cook for 5 minutes, stirring occasionally.

2. Add white wine, Pernod if desired, lemon juice, fennel seeds, oregano, and clams. Cover, reduce heat slightly, and simmer just until clams open, shaking pan occasionally.

3. Ladle clams and broth into four serving bowls, discarding any clams that do not open, sprinkle with basil slivers, and serve immediately.

SERVES 4
APPROXIMATELY 2.2 GRAMS FAT PER SERVING

♦ ♦ ♦ ♦ ♦

SPINACH RAITA

▶▶▶▶▶▶▶▶▶▶▶▶▶▶▶▶▶▶▶▶▶▶▶▶

Raita is often served as a cooling accompaniment to curried and other highly spiced Indian dishes. My low fat Spinach Raita is ideal for that purpose, but it is tasty enough to be served on its own as a first course. It also makes an excellent dip or spread.

6   ounces fresh spinach, trimmed
1   medium cucumber, peeled, seeded, and coarsely
    chopped
2   cups low fat plain yogurt
1   teaspoon ground cumin
1/4 teaspoon ground cardamom
    Salt and freshly ground pepper to taste
    Mild or hot paprika to taste

1. Rinse spinach well and shake off water. Place in a large pot, cover, and steam over medium heat for 3 or 4 minutes or until wilted. Remove from heat, transfer spinach to a colander to drain, and cool to room temperature. When cool, lightly squeeze out any remaining liquid and chop spinach finely—there should be about 1/2 cup.

2. While spinach cools, place cucumber on paper towels to allow excess liquid to drain.

3. In a mixing bowl, blend yogurt with cumin, cardamom, and salt and pepper. Add cucumber and spinach and

stir until ingredients are well blended. Cover and refrigerate for at least 2 hours. Sprinkle lightly with paprika before serving.

MAKES ABOUT 3 CUPS
APPROXIMATELY .8 GRAM FAT PER ¼ CUP

◆ ◆ ◆ ◆ ◆

TOMATO OLIVE CROSTINI

▶ ▶

The first time I tasted this luscious antipasto was in a quaint northern Italian restaurant some years ago. It was dressed with incredible amounts of both oil and olives, but I have found that skimping on these two ingredients has not meant skimping on taste one bit.

If you happen to have a little sauce left over, boil up some pasta, stir it in, and enjoy!

1   *teaspoon olive oil*

1   *cup coarsely chopped plum tomatoes, fresh or no-salt-added canned, peeled, and drained*

1   *tablespoon chopped fresh oregano or 1 teaspoon dried*

1   *tablespoon chopped fresh parsley*

3   *black olives, preferably Gaeta, pitted and coarsely chopped*

2   *teaspoons capers, rinsed and drained*

1/8   *teaspoon hot red pepper flakes, or to taste*

1   *small clove garlic, pressed or finely minced*

1   *tablespoon full-bodied red wine (optional)*

8   *slices Italian bread, about 1/2-inch-thick each, cut from a large round (10-inch-diameter) loaf*

1   *whole clove garlic, peeled*

1. Combine all ingredients except bread and whole garlic clove in medium bowl and stir to blend. Let stand at room temperature for at least 1 hour to blend flavors. (At this point,

mixture can be refrigerated for up to 4 hours, but return to room temperature before serving.)

2. Toast or grill Italian bread slices until golden. While bread is still hot, slice garlic clove in half, rub each slice of bread quickly with the cut side of the garlic, and top with about 2 tablespoons of the tomato mixture. Cut each crostini in half and serve.

MAKES 16 PIECES OR 8 SERVINGS
APPROXIMATELY 1.4 GRAMS FAT PER SERVING

◆ ◆ ◆ ◆ ◆

SHERRIED LENTIL SPREAD

▶ ▶

Serve this tasty spread with hearty whole-grain crackers or thinly sliced bread.

2	teaspoons vegetable oil
1	medium-large Spanish onion, chopped
1/4	cup Low Fat Chicken Broth (page 43) or canned low-sodium broth
1	clove garlic, quartered
2 1/2	cups cooked lentils
2	tablespoons cream sherry
1/4	teaspoon nutmeg
	Salt and freshly ground pepper to taste

1. Heat oil in large nonstick skillet and sauté onion over medium-low heat, stirring frequently, until onion is wilted. Add broth and garlic, raise heat to medium and continue to cook, stirring, until onion is very soft and liquid is reduced.

2. Combine onion and garlic mixture with lentils in food processor and pulse on and off, scraping down sides often, until mixture is chunky but not pureed.

3. Add sherry, nutmeg, and salt and pepper and process briefly; mixture should retain a chunky texture. Chill slightly before serving.

MAKES ABOUT 2 1/2 CUPS
APPROXIMATELY .3 GRAM FAT PER TABLESPOON

SAUTÉED WILD MUSHROOMS

► ►

M y friend Josephine speaks so lovingly about her immigrant father, Joe, that I share her wistful memories. "A man of the earth," she says proudly. She recounts how he stomped on grapes to produce a "very heady" wine, pressed olives producing a "verdant fruity" olive oil, preserved fruits and pickled fresh garden vegetables "sharp as a serpent's tooth," and enjoyed a certain reputation in the wilderness for "knowing about fungi."

Papa Joe was a mycologist without the benefit of book learning. He could identify mushrooms and discern the toxic ones through careful examination of their spores. "Very important," Josephine reminds me.

Papa Joe would return from his hunt before lunchtime bringing baskets filled with his treasures. After dusting off any clinging debris, he plunged them into a kettle containing a small amount of boiling water and a handful of shiny new silver coins. Toxic mushrooms would tarnish the silver, Josephine explains. A contaminated batch, thus deemed poisonous, was tossed. Otherwise, the mushrooms were gently lifted from their bath for proper cooking. Josephine never recalled her father discarding even one of his prizes. "And I'm still here, aren't I?" she says, living proof of his expertise. She assures me that her father would have loved my version of sautéed wild mushrooms.

I do not advise picking your own mushrooms and testing them with silver coins, especially since a wide variety of wild, nontoxic mushrooms can now be found at many greengrocers and supermarkets. Although almost any kind of wild mushroom can be used for this dish, if there's a selection, choose the mildly flavored fresh oyster mushrooms.

> 2 teaspoons olive oil
> 1 small clove garlic, minced
> ³/₄ pound fresh oyster mushrooms or other wild mushrooms, wiped clean, cut into large pieces
> 1 small dried hot red pepper pod, unbroken
> 3 tablespoons Low Fat Chicken Broth (page 43) or canned low-sodium broth
> ¹/₂ cup dry white wine
> ¹/₄ cup chopped fresh parsley
> Assorted wild greens (such as watercress, arugula, young dandelion greens, or chicory), trimmed, rinsed, and drained
> Juice of one large lemon
> Coarse salt and freshly ground pepper to taste

1. Heat oil in large nonstick skillet and sauté garlic over medium heat, stirring, for about 2 minutes or until softened.

2. Add mushrooms and hot pepper pod and swirl quickly in pan. Raise heat to medium-high, add broth, and cook, swirling mushrooms gently, for 2 minutes.

3. Pour in wine and simmer, continuing to swirl mushrooms in pan for another 4 to 5 minutes or until wine is reduced and mushrooms are wilted. Discard pepper pod and stir in parsley.

4. Arrange greens on flat salad plates, top with portions of mushrooms and any liquid, sprinkle with fresh lemon

juice, a grinding or two of black pepper, and a sprinkle of coarse salt if desired. Serve immediately.

SERVES 4
APPROXIMATELY 2.7 GRAMS FAT PER SERVING

♦ ♦ ♦ ♦ ♦

TINY POTATOES WITH CAVIAR

▶ ▶

For me, caviar is a comfort food I find difficult to give up completely. There's no denying it, caviar is expensive—in fat, cholesterol, and sodium, as well as in price. In very small portions, however, such as in this precursor to a festive meal, caviar can be an acceptable special-occasion indulgence that turns any gathering into a party.

12   *tiny new potatoes (preferably no larger than 1¹/₂ inches in diameter), rinsed*

2   *tablespoons light sour cream*

2   *tablespoons low fat (1%) milk*

2   *tablespoons finely minced fresh chives*

    Salt and white pepper to taste

1   *ounce caviar (red, black, or golden)*

1. Preheat oven to 350°F.

2. Bake potatoes for 15 to 20 minutes or until tender.

3. Cut potatoes in half and scoop out pulp, taking care not to break the skins. Transfer pulp to a medium bowl and set skins aside.

4. Whip potato pulp with sour cream, milk, chives, and salt and pepper to taste.

5. Spoon mixture back into potato shells and top each with a hint of caviar.

MAKES 24 POTATO HALVES

APPROXIMATELY .3 GRAM FAT PER POTATO HALF

◆ ◆ ◆ ◆ ◆

CREAMED TUNA
WITH GREEN PEPPERCORNS

▶ ▶

This versatile dip can be served with crudités, crackers, or toasted pita triangles. It also makes a delicious stuffing—try it in cherry tomatoes, hollowed-out cucumbers, or hard cooked egg-white halves, topped with minced fresh parsley or chopped chives.

1	6¹/₈-ounce can light water-packed tuna, drained
¹/₂	cup low fat plain yogurt
2	tablespoons light sour cream
2	tablespoons light mayonnaise
¹/₂	small onion, chopped
2	dashes Worcestershire sauce
1	tablespoon no-salt-added tomato paste
1¹/₂	teaspoons green peppercorns (rinsed and drained if salt-coated or packed in brine)
	Salt to taste

Combine all ingredients except salt in a blender or food processor and process until smooth and creamy. Taste and add salt, if desired.

MAKES ABOUT 1¹/₂ CUPS

APPROXIMATELY .6 GRAM FAT PER TABLESPOON

◆ ◆ ◆ ◆ ◆

SALMON CUCUMBER MOUSSE

▶ ▶

$\mathbb{M}$y salmon cucumber mousse is a breeze to prepare and a joy to eat. If you're using canned salmon, opt for the red variety; the pink just doesn't have the same rich full taste.

 2 *tablespoons cold water*
 1 *packet unflavored gelatin*
 1/3 *cup boiling water*
 3/4 *pound salmon fillet, cooked, skinned, and flaked, or 14³/4-ounce can red salmon, bones and skin removed*
 1 *small onion, quartered*
 1 *small cucumber, peeled, quartered, and seeded*
 1/2 *cup low fat plain yogurt*
 1/4 *cup light sour cream*
 2 *teaspoons chopped fresh dill*
   Salt and freshly ground pepper to taste
 1 *sprig fresh dill for garnish*

1. Pour cold water into the work bowl of a food processor, sprinkle with gelatin, and let stand 5 minutes. Add boiling water and process quickly with a few on/off motions until gelatin is dissolved.

2. Add salmon, onion, cucumber, yogurt, sour cream, and chopped dill and process, scraping sides down frequently, until mixture is smooth and creamy. Season to taste with salt and pepper.

3. Transfer mixture to a decorative serving bowl, lay dill sprig lightly on top, cover and refrigerate for several hours or overnight. This mousse can be prepared a day ahead if kept well covered and chilled.

MAKES ABOUT 2½ CUPS
APPROXIMATELY 1.0 GRAM FAT PER TABLESPOON

◆ ◆ ◆ ◆ ◆

HUMMUS NO TAHINI

▶ ▶

One of my greatest joys is playing backgammon, poker, Trivial Pursuit, or Scrabble. And it's not uncommon to have a "play for blood" game going several times a year. Dinner with game enthusiasts who also happen to be friends can be a tricky piece of business to plan. Generally, I get the ball rolling with a tray of lushly appointed appetizers as a peace offering. And win or lose, this dip keeps everyone happy.

You will note there is no tahini in this hummus recipe. For, though it is absolutely delicious, the rich (about 8 grams of fat per tablespoon) sesame paste can add inches to the hips just by reading its name.

Serve with pita triangles or a bouquet of colorful raw or blanched vegetables.

  1 *cup cooked or canned chick-peas, rinsed, drained*
 1/4 *cup Low Fat Chicken Broth (page 43) or canned*
     low-sodium broth
 1/2 *cup low fat plain yogurt*
  2 *medium cloves garlic, cut in half*
     Juice of 1 large lemon, or more to taste
     Salt and freshly ground pepper to taste

Combine all ingredients, except salt and pepper, in the work bowl of a food processor and process until mixture is smooth, scraping down the sides of the bowl as necessary.

Taste and correct seasonings, transfer to a bowl, and serve.

<small>MAKES ABOUT 2 CUPS</small>
<small>APPROXIMATELY .2 GRAM FAT PER TABLESPOON</small>

◆ ◆ ◆ ◆ ◆

EGGPLANT PUREE

▶ ▶

Also called poor man's caviar, this popular Mideastern dish makes a delicious spread (especially good with heated whole-wheat pita), and is perfect as a dip for fresh raw or crisp-steamed vegetables.

2   *small eggplants, about ³/₄ pound each*
1   *small onion, chopped*
2   *cloves garlic, chopped*
2   *tablespoons chopped fresh parsley*
     Salt and freshly ground pepper to taste
3   *tablespoons fresh lemon juice, or more to taste*
     Paprika or minced fresh parsley for garnish

1. Preheat oven to 450°F.

2. Pierce eggplants in several places with a sharp fork and place on a nonstick baking pan. Roast, turning once during cooking, for about 40 minutes or until eggplants are very soft. Remove from oven, make a small slit down center of each eggplant to allow steam to escape, and let stand until cool enough to handle.

3. Cut off stems and cut eggplants in half lengthwise. Scoop out pulp and discard skins. Place pulp in a colander or strainer over sink or bowl to drain bitter liquid. Press down gently to extract as much excess liquid as possible.

4. Combine eggplant pulp with remaining ingredients in the work bowl of a food processor or blender and process until smooth.

---

5. Transfer to a decorative bowl and serve chilled or at room temperature, sprinkled lightly with paprika or minced parsley.

MAKES ABOUT 2¼ CUPS
LESS THAN .1 GRAM FAT PER TABLESPOON

◆ ◆ ◆ ◆ ◆

CHICKEN YAKITORI

▶ ▶

Fun to eat and a recipe that lends itself beautifully to outdoor entertaining, yakitori on skewers can be anything from beef to seafood to vegetables. The important thing is the marinade, which obviates the need for a sauce, spicy or otherwise. Serve with fresh lemon wedges.

2¹/₂   *tablespoons sugar or honey*
  ¹/₂   *cup mirin (available at health food or specialty stores)*
    2   *tablespoons low-sodium soy sauce*
  ¹/₂   *cup sake (rice wine) or dry white wine*
  ¹/₂   *cup Low Fat Chicken Broth (page 43) or canned low-sodium broth*
    1   *whole skinless, boneless chicken breast (about ¹/₂ pound), halved and trimmed of all visible fat*
   12   *bamboo skewers soaked in water 30 minutes*
    2   *medium leeks, white part only, rinsed and cut into 1¹/₂-inch lengths (try to keep the rounds whole)*
    2   *medium green bell peppers, seeded and cut into 2-inch strips lengthwise and then cut in half crosswise.*
       Juice of 1 lemon

1. Preheat broiler or prepare grill.

2. Combine sugar or honey, mirin, soy sauce, sake, and broth in small saucepan and bring to a boil. Reduce heat

immediately and simmer for about 10 minutes or until reduced by about ¼. Set sauce aside.

3. Rinse chicken under cold water. Drain, pat dry, and cut into 1-inch cubes. Thread chicken pieces on skewers, alternating with leek and green pepper segments.

4. Grill or broil unsauced chicken and vegetables briefly, turning to brown lightly on all sides, then brush with sauce and return to the grill or broiler. Repeat procedure three more times, cooking the kebabs only briefly on all sides each time, until chicken is cooked through but not dry.

5. Lay skewers on a platter and sprinkle immediately with fresh lemon juice. Serve hot or warm.

SERVES 4

APPROXIMATELY 1.0 GRAM FAT PER SERVING

SOUPS
and
CHOWDERS

◆ ◆ ◆ ◆

LOW FAT CHICKEN BROTH

▶ ▶

This flavorful broth can be served on its own, or used as a stock for soups, dressings, sauces, or whatever. I use it for almost all my low fat soups because I can control the quantity of salt. Although most good canned broths are low in fat they often contain large amounts of sodium.

The broth can be frozen in serving-size containers until ready to use.

1	pound chicken scraps (backs, wings, necks)
8	cups water
1/2	cup dry white wine
	Salt to taste
10	whole peppercorns or 1/2 teaspoon freshly ground pepper
1	large onion, chopped
2	large carrots, chopped
2	large celery stalks, with tops, chopped
1	clove garlic, quartered
1	bay leaf
1	teaspoon dried thyme
1/2	teaspoon dried marjoram
6	sprigs parsley
1	cup cooked rice or noodles (optional)

1. Place all ingredients, except rice or noodles, in a large stockpot and bring to a boil. Cover, reduce heat to very low, and simmer for about 2 hours. Remove broth from heat and cool to room temperature.

---

2. Pour broth through a fine strainer or sieve lined with cheesecloth into a large bowl, pressing lightly on solids to extract liquid. Discard solids.

3. Cover broth and refrigerate for 2 to 3 hours or until well chilled. Skim off all hardened surface fat and discard.

4. Reheat broth, adding rice or noodles if desired, and serve. Or transfer broth to serving-size containers, cover, date, and freeze for future use.

MAKES APPROXIMATELY 6 CUPS
APPROXIMATELY 1.0 GRAM FAT PER CUP

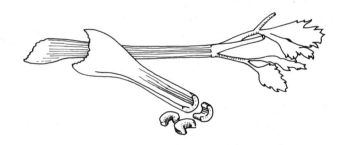

SPLIT PEA
AND SMOKED TURKEY SOUP

▶ ▶

This is a low fat version of one of my favorite soups. The smoked turkey I use here successfully mimics the rich smoky flavor of fat-hearty ham hocks used in traditional split pea soup recipes. However, because smoked turkey is somewhat salty (this soup contains 440 milligrams sodium per serving), don't be tempted to add any additional salt until tasting the soup just before serving.

I often double the recipe and keep extra containers handy in my freezer throughout the winter. For me, nothing is as comforting as having a steaming bowl for lunch on a cold day or with leftovers-filled sandwiches as a light, satisfying dinner.

A nice garnish for this soup would be shredded lettuce cooked briefly in a little chicken broth.

$^1/_2$ cup green split peas, picked over and rinsed
1   medium onion, coarsely chopped
1   large carrot, diced
1   large stalk celery, thinly sliced
1   large clove garlic, minced
2   cups Low Fat Chicken Broth (page 43) or canned
     low-sodium broth
3   cups water
6   ounces smoked turkey breast, unsliced
     Coarsely ground pepper to taste

1. In a large soup pot, combine all ingredients, except 1 cup of water, turkey, and pepper. Bring to a boil, reduce heat, and simmer gently for 1½ hours or until peas are nearly cooked. Stir occasionally and check fluid level. If necessary, add additional water, ¼ cup at a time. Soup should be fairly thick.

2. When peas are nearly tender, add turkey in one piece, cover, and simmer for 15 minutes or until turkey is heated through.

3. Remove turkey, dice and shred or tear it into small pieces. (If desired, soup can be pureed in a food processor at this point, although I prefer the variety of colors and chunky texture.) Return turkey pieces to pot (if soup has been pureed, return to pot with turkey and keep heat low), and heat through.

4. Before serving, stir in several grindings of pepper.

SERVES 4

APPROXIMATELY 3.3 GRAMS FAT PER SERVING

◆ ◆ ◆ ◆ ◆

WILD RICE BISQUE

▶ ▶

As you probably know, wild rice is not really rice at all, but a long-grain marsh grass indigenous to the northern Great Lakes area of North America where it is often harvested by local Native Americans. It requires a thorough cleaning before cooking and, depending on the method used, a relatively long cooking time (in general, it's best to follow directions on the package because overcooking can produce starchy results).

Revered for its rich nutty flavor and chewy texture, wild rice stands up majestically to the aromatic flavors it cooks with in this eye-pleasing, delicious soup.

  2 teaspoons olive oil
  2 large shallots, minced
  3 large cloves garlic, minced (optional)
  2 tablespoons flour
  3 cups Low Fat Chicken Broth (page 43) or canned
     low-sodium broth
  1 cup water
1½ cups diced carrots
1½ cups cooked wild rice
 ¾ cup nonfat dry milk
     Salt and freshly ground pepper to taste

1. Heat oil in a nonstick pot (I use a large stir-fry pan with a handle) and sauté shallots and garlic over low heat, stirring often, until shallots are translucent.

2. Sprinkle with flour and stir to dissolve, stir in ¼ cup broth or water and raise heat to medium. Cook for about 2 minutes.

3. Add remaining broth and water, carrots, and rice. Sprinkle with nonfat dry milk and stir well, then add generous grindings of pepper. Cover and cook over very low heat, stirring occasionally, for about 20 minutes or until carrots are tender—do not allow soup to boil. Add extra water, ¼ cup at a time, if too much liquid evaporates. Taste and add salt, if desired.

SERVES 4
APPROXIMATELY 5.2 GRAMS FAT PER SERVING

◆ ◆ ◆ ◆ ◆

SAFFRON FISH SOUP

▶ ▶

This very luxurious dish is a lovely mix of finfish and seafood delicately flavored with the most precious spice in the world: saffron.

Saffron is the yellow-orange stigma of a variety of the crocus. Each crocus flower yields but three, which must be handpicked and then set out to dry. It takes more than 14,000 of these tiny stigmas to produce one ounce of saffron. Although it comes to supermarkets and specialty food stores in both powdered form and in threads, the powdered variety loses its flavor more readily and can be easily adulterated by less expensive imitations. There's really no substitute for the aromatic pungency—in bouillabaisse, paella, and a number of other classically turned-out dishes, and fortunately, a little goes a long way. Threads should be crushed just before using and stored in an airtight container in a cool dark place.

    1   tablespoon olive oil
    1   small onion, chopped
    1   leek, white and pale greens, chopped
    2   large cloves garlic, chopped
    1   tablespoon no-salt-added tomato paste
    1   pound mixed fish fillets (hake, red snapper,
        haddock, cod, or scrod), cut into large pieces
  1/4   pound scallops, rinsed, large scallops cut in half
  1/4   pound medium shrimp, shelled and deveined
    2   cups Low Fat Chicken Broth (page 43) or canned
        low-sodium broth

        1   cup bottled clam juice
      ¹/₂   teaspoon crushed saffron threads
        1   cup water, heated
      ¹/₂   cup chopped fresh parsley
            Salt and freshly ground pepper
            Fresh basil slivers
        6   slices French bread, toasted and rubbed with
            garlic

1. Heat oil in a pot and sauté onion, leek, and garlic over low heat, stirring frequently, until wilted but not browned. Stir in tomato paste and cook for 2 minutes.
2. Lay in fish, scallops, and shrimp, and pour in broth and clam juice. Mix saffron with heated water, set aside for five minutes, then add to pot, stirring lightly to blend.
3. Cover and cook over very low heat for 15 minutes or until fish is tender. Taste and add salt and pepper, if desired.
4. Ladle into warmed bowls, dividing fish equally, sprinkle with basil, and serve accompanied by toasted bread.

SERVES 6

APPROXIMATELY 4.9 GRAMS FAT PER SERVING

◆ ◆ ◆ ◆ ◆

SHRIMP AND CRABMEAT CHOWDER

▶ ▶

I'm mad for chowder. Especially the creamy variety. But I'm madder still at the fat content of the cream. The traditional recipe for a seafood chowder calls for three or four slices of salt pork or bacon and about two cups of cream, along with the fish, seafood, vegetables, and other ingredients. My low fat version produces the same desirable "creaminess." In fact, I think this chowder comes as close to the rich, comforting taste of the real McCoy as you can get without the fat—or the remorse.

You may wish to stir in a pinch of thyme just before you ladle it up and dust the top of each bowl with a bit of paprika for color. This marvelous chowder deserves the featured place on any luncheon or supper menu.

2	*cups water*
	Salt
1/2	*pound shrimp in shell, rinsed*
1	*cup clam juice*
2	*large shallots, diced*
2	*medium potatoes, peeled and cut into 1-inch cubes*
1	*large stalk celery, diced*
1	*medium carrot, diced*
1	*tablespoon chopped fresh parsley*
	Freshly ground pepper to taste
	Pinch cayenne
1/2	*pound fresh, canned, or frozen crabmeat, picked over*

1   tablespoon flour
1½ cups low fat (1%) milk
    Thyme and paprika to taste

1. In a large saucepan, bring water and a pinch of salt to a boil, add shrimp, and cook for 5 minutes. Remove shrimp, reserving water. Set shrimp aside to cool slightly.

2. Add clam juice, shallots, potatoes, celery, carrot, parsley, salt and pepper, and cayenne to water in saucepan. Cover and simmer gently for 15 minutes.

3. Shell and devein shrimp and cut into ½-inch pieces. Add shrimp and crabmeat to vegetables.

4. Stir flour into milk until thoroughly blended and add to saucepan. Cook, stirring, over medium heat for 5 minutes, but do not let the soup boil. Stir in thyme and sprinkle with paprika, if desired. Serve immediately.

SERVES 4

APPROXIMATELY 2.6 GRAMS FAT PER SERVING

◆ ◆ ◆ ◆ ◆

VEGETABLE RICE SOUP

▶ ▶

Here is a heartening soup that will lie gently on the stomach and help chase the blues away. It is composed of the best fresh vegetables the summer has to offer, and they blend wonderfully well with each other without losing their individuality.

1	tablespoon olive or vegetable oil
1	large green bell pepper, cored, seeded, and chopped
1	small zucchini, sliced
1	small yellow squash, sliced
1	medium onion, chopped
2	cloves garlic, minced
1/2	pound mushrooms, wiped clean, trimmed, and sliced
1	tablespoon no-salt-added tomato paste
4	large ripe tomatoes, peeled and chopped, juice reserved
1/2	teaspoon dried thyme
1/2	teaspoon dried basil
1 1/2	cups Low Fat Chicken Broth (page 43) or canned low sodium broth
1/2	cup dry white wine
	Salt and freshly ground pepper to taste
2	cups warm cooked brown rice

1. Heat oil in large stockpot over medium-low heat and sauté green pepper, zucchini, yellow squash, onion, garlic,

and mushrooms, stirring frequently, for about 10 minutes or until softened. Stir in tomato paste and cook for 2 minutes more.

2. Add tomatoes with any accumulated juice, thyme, basil, broth, and wine, raise heat and bring to a boil. Reduce heat, cover, and cook for 20 minutes.

3. Taste and season with salt and pepper, if desired. Divide rice among warmed bowls, add soup, and serve immediately.

SERVES 4
APPROXIMATELY 6.6 GRAMS FAT PER SERVING

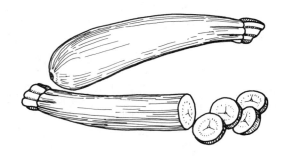

◆ ◆ ◆ ◆ ◆

SPANISH CHICK-PEA SOUP
(POTAJE DE GARBANZOS)

▶ ▶

The first time I tasted this soup I didn't relish it at all. As is the custom in any well-ordered Spanish or Mexican lunch or dinner, it was served as the second course of a rather large meal. The waiter brought out a hearty soup, heavy with pork fat, which led to the Mother of All Upset Stomachs. Along with the ancient and honored legume, the garbanzo, the potaje included bay leaves, onion, cloves, salt and pepper, and the yolks of hard-cooked eggs. The soup was accompanied by greasy fried bread.

With time, subsequent visits to better Spanish and Mexican restaurants, and through my acquaintances with home cooks of Spanish descent, I have become an aficionado. Serve this thick soup as a first course or as a light but filling supper accompanied by garlicky toasted pita wedges and a green salad.

1	teaspoon vegetable oil
2	medium onions, chopped
3	large cloves garlic, chopped, or to taste
2	cups no-salt-added plum tomatoes, undrained, chopped
2	cups chick-peas, cooked or canned, rinsed and drained
1	large carrot, diced
1/4	cup chopped fresh parsley
	Freshly ground pepper
2	cups water

$^1/_4$ *pound Italian-flavored turkey sausage, boiled,*
      drained, and cut in chunks
$^3/_4$ *cup diced lean (95% fat free), cooked ham*
  2   *large potatoes, peeled and cubed*
  1   *bay leaf*
  1   *pound escarole, well rinsed and trimmed,*
      coarsely chopped
      Salt to taste

1. Heat oil in large stockpot over low heat. Cook onions and garlic, stirring frequently, until onions are wilted. If mixture begins to stick, add a few tablespoons water.

2. Add tomatoes with juice, chick-peas, carrot, parsley, several grindings of pepper, and water. Bring to a boil, reduce heat, and simmer, covered, for $^1/_2$ hour or until vegetables are tender.

3. Remove from heat, puree mixture in a food processor, and return to pot. Add sausage, ham, diced potatoes, bay leaf, escarole, and additional water if necessary. Soup should be thick but not pasty. Cover and simmer for 15 minutes or until potatoes are tender and ham and sausage are heated through. Taste and correct seasonings.

SERVES **4**
APPROXIMATELY **8.8** GRAMS FAT PER SERVING

◆ ◆ ◆ ◆ ◆

DILLED CARROT SOUP

▶ ▶

Give me a handful of carrots and I have no more culinary problems. Not only do I dote on Bugs Bunny's favorite vegetable, I find it compatible with practically everything in my cooking repertoire.

My lovely dill-flavored carrot soup doesn't disguise the unique character of carrot; rather it coaxes out and exploits its true flavor. I adore it served plain or garnished with sliced scallions, and a dollop of low fat yogurt, as here.

	Vegetable oil cooking spray
2	*medium leeks, white and tender greens, rinsed well and thinly sliced*
2	*cups Low Fat Chicken Broth (page 43), or canned low-sodium broth*
1½	*cups thinly sliced carrots*
½	*cup water*
⅛	*teaspoon salt, or to taste*
2	*teaspoons minced fresh dillweed or 1 teaspoon dried*
⅛	*teaspoon black pepper, or to taste*
2	*tablespoons low fat plain yogurt*
2	*scallions, white and tender greens, thinly sliced*

1. Coat a nonstick pot with cooking spray and heat gently. Add leeks and sauté over medium heat for about 5 minutes or until tender. If mixture begins to stick, add 2 tablespoons broth. Add remaining broth, carrots, water, salt,

dill, and pepper and bring to a boil. Cover, reduce heat, and simmer for 15 to 20 minutes or until vegetables are tender.

2. Puree carrot mixture in thirds and return puree to saucepan. Cook over medium flame until heated, stirring occasionally. Ladle soup into individual serving bowls and top each serving with 1/2 tablespoon yogurt and a sprinkling of sliced scallions.

SERVES 4

APPROXIMATELY 2.4 GRAMS FAT PER SERVING

◆ ◆ ◆ ◆ ◆

ACORN SQUASH AND APPLE SOUP

▶ ▶

It seems just about everybody everywhere is interested in lighter, more imaginative cuisine that will satisfy not only the epicurean but also average folks who want to eat tasty food without feeling as though they've sinned. This savory, slightly sweet squash soup fills the bill nicely. Hearty enough for the chilly days of autumn, it is a perfect prelude to any holiday dinner.

1	large acorn squash
	Vegetable oil cooking spray
2	medium onions, chopped
1	stalk celery, chopped
2	cups Low Fat Chicken Broth (page 43), or canned low-sodium broth
2	cooking apples, peeled, cored, and chopped
2	small potatoes, peeled and diced
1	cup apple juice
2	tablespoons fresh lemon juice
	Salt and freshly ground pepper to taste
¹/₄	teaspoon ground cinnamon, or to taste
¹/₄	teaspoon ground nutmeg, or to taste
1	cup low fat (1%) milk
	Paprika

1. Preheat oven to 350°F.
2. Cut squash in half, remove seeds, and place squash, cut side down, on a baking pan sprayed with cooking oil.

Cover and bake for 1 hour or until soft. Remove from oven and let cool slightly.

3. Meanwhile, combine onions and celery in a nonstick pot sprayed with cooking oil. Cook over low heat, stirring often, for 5 minutes or until onions are translucent. If mixture begins to stick, add a few tablespoons of broth.

4. Add broth, apples, potatoes, apple juice, and lemon juice to pot and stir gently. Bring to a boil, then cover, reduce heat, and simmer gently for 15 minutes or until potatoes are tender. Season to taste with salt, pepper, cinnamon, and nutmeg.

5. Discarding skin, scoop out pulp from half of the squash and place in a food processor with half of the milk. Process until smooth, transfer to pot with soup, then repeat with remaining pulp and milk.

6. Cook soup, stirring constantly, over low heat until it is hot but not boiling. Ladle into soup plates, sprinkle lightly with paprika, and serve.

SERVES 4

APPROXIMATELY 3.0 GRAMS FAT PER SERVING

♦ ♦ ♦ ♦ ♦

CREAM OF ASPARAGUS SOUP

▶ ▶

My version of Cream of Asparagus Soup may be slimmed down, but it's far from skimpy. It relies on the delicate flavor of the asparagus itself rather than masking it in a dense cloud of cream.

I sometimes substitute two cups of diced celery for the asparagus or prepare it with a pound and a half of cauliflower (stems and florets), romaine, or iceberg lettuce.

1½   *pounds asparagus*
2   *medium onions, chopped*
2   *cups water*
2   *cups Low Fat Chicken Broth (page 43) or canned low-sodium broth*
2   *teaspoons chopped fresh dillweed or 1 teaspoon dried*
1   *teaspoon dried thyme*
     Salt and freshly ground pepper to taste
1   *tablespoon flour*
1½   *cups low fat (1%) milk*

1. Snap off tough asparagus stems and discard. Break off asparagus tips and set aside. Chop remaining stems coarsely.

2. Combine chopped asparagus stems with all remaining ingredients, except flour and milk, in a large pot. Bring to a boil, then reduce heat to very low, cover, and cook for 10 minutes or until asparagus is tender. Remove from heat and cool slightly.

3. Transfer cooled soup, a cup at a time, to a food processor and process until smooth. Return pureed soup to pot, add asparagus tips, and cook over very low heat for 2 minutes.

4. Dissolve flour in milk and add to soup. Continue to cook over very low heat, stirring constantly, until soup is slightly thickened and heated through—do not boil. Transfer to a tureen or individual bowls and serve immediately.

SERVES 4

APPROXIMATELY 2.6 GRAMS FAT PER SERVING

MEATS

◆ ◆ ◆ ◆ ◆

BEEF À LA BOURGUIGNONNE

▶ ▶

B*eef à la Bourguignonne* means, of course, beef cooked in the style of one of France's great gastronomic regions, Burgundy, with the robust, dry red wine of that region.

This basic and delicious stew is a meal-in-one-pot that my family and friends always enjoy. One big selling point is that it practically cooks itself. After briefly searing the meat to lock in its juices, slowly stew or braise the beef in its savory Burgundy-based cooking liquid. This provides ample time for you to relax and chat with your dinner guests. Because it reheats so beautifully, you can even prepare it a day or two in advance.

This hearty entrée needs nothing else save a simple salad on the side, some warm French bread, and a robust bottle of Burgundy.

2	teaspoons vegetable oil
³/₄	pound beef top round, trimmed of all visible fat and cut into 1-inch cubes
1	dozen small white onions
2	tablespoons plus 1 cup low sodium beef broth
3	cloves garlic, minced
2	tablespoons flour
2	teaspoons dried rosemary
1	teaspoon dried thyme
	Salt and freshly ground pepper to taste
2	cups Burgundy or other full-bodied dry red wine
16	tiny new potatoes, peeled
1	cup diced carrots

$^3/_4$ *pound very large mushrooms, wiped clean and halved*

1. Preheat oven to 275°F.
2. Heat oil in a large ovenproof pot or casserole. Add beef and brown over medium-high heat, removing the pieces as they are done. Do not crowd meat or it won't brown properly.
3. When beef has browned, transfer it to a platter and keep warm. Lower heat to medium-low, add onions and 2 tablespoons broth to pot, and cook, stirring, for 2 minutes. Add garlic and cook for an additional 3 minutes.
4. Return beef to pot and sprinkle with flour. Stir until flour is dissolved. Add rosemary, thyme, salt and pepper, wine, and remaining broth. Cover and bake in preheated oven for about 2 hours. Check after an hour and add a little water or wine if too much liquid has evaporated.
5. Add potatoes, carrots, and mushrooms to pot, cover, return to oven, and cook an additional hour or until vegetables are tender. Taste and adjust seasonings, if necessary.

SERVES 4
APPROXIMATELY 7.8 GRAMS FAT PER SERVING

◆ ◆ ◆ ◆

STIR-FRIED STEAK
WITH ASPARAGUS

▶ ▶

$\mathbb{S}$tir-frying is a technique for quick-cooking small pieces of food in a wok or skillet over high heat while constantly and vigorously stirring. Long used by Oriental cooks, stir-frying fits right into our scheme of things because it requires little fat and the results are always crisp and tender.

3/4	*pound top round, trimmed of all visible fat and cut into 1/4-inch strips*
3	*tablespoons dry white wine*
2	*tablespoons low sodium soy sauce*
1	*clove garlic, finely minced*
1	*teaspoon freshly grated ginger root*
1	*pound asparagus*
2	*teaspoons vegetable oil*
1/2	*cup canned water chestnuts, drained*
6	*scallions, white and tender greens, sliced*
1	*teaspoon cornstarch*
2	*tablespoons water*
1	*tablespoon chopped fresh parsley*

1. Put beef in a bowl. Combine wine with soy sauce, garlic, and ginger root and pour over beef. Toss lightly and marinate at room temperature for 30 minutes.

2. Break off and discard tough stems of asparagus. Cut asparagus in half lengthwise, then slice asparagus crosswise into 1 1/2-inch pieces.

3. Heat oil in a large nonstick wok or skillet. Add asparagus and stir over high heat for 1 minute. Add water chestnuts and scallions. Stir an additional minute. With a slotted spoon, remove vegetables to a heated bowl.

4. Add beef and its marinade to skillet. Stir over high heat for 1 minute or until meat loses its raw color. With a slotted spoon transfer meat to bowl with vegetables.

5. Dissolve cornstarch in water and add to skillet. Cook over high heat for 30 seconds or until sauce starts to thicken. Return vegetables and meat to skillet and stir just until heated through. Transfer contents of skillet to serving dish, sprinkle with parsley, and serve.

SERVES 4
APPROXIMATELY 7.6 GRAMS FAT PER SERVING

◆ ◆ ◆ ◆ ◆

HERBED MEAT LOAF

▶ ▶

Meat loaf of any kind heads my list of comfort foods. In fact, I enjoy it so much that I usually double the recipe, cook both loaves, then wrap and freeze one for another meal.

I usually prepare this dish with long-grain white rice but if you prefer brown rice, the loaf will have a grainier texture and nuttier flavor.

Good accompaniments are Creamy Whipped Potatoes (page 171), Mushroom and Onion Gravy (page 8), and braised endive.

   $^1/_2$ cup Thick and Rich Tomato Sauce (page 3) or canned low sodium tomato sauce

   1   teaspoon sugar

   1   teaspoon chopped fresh oregano or $^1/_2$ teaspoon dried

   1   teaspoon chopped fresh thyme or $^1/_2$ teaspoon dried

   $^3/_4$ pound lean ground light-meat turkey

   $^1/_2$ pound very lean ground pork

   1   large clove garlic, pressed or finely minced

   $^1/_4$ onion, finely chopped

   2   tablespoons minced fresh parsley
       White of 1 large egg

   $^1/_4$ cup cooked rice
       Salt and freshly ground pepper to taste

1. Preheat oven to 350°F.

2. In small bowl, combine tomato sauce with sugar, oregano, and thyme, and set aside.

3. In a large bowl, combine turkey, pork, garlic, onion, parsley, egg white, and rice. Add tomato sauce mixture and blend gently with hands, then taste and add salt and pepper.

4. Mold into loaf shape and place on an ungreased baking sheet or in a shallow pan. Cook in center of preheated oven for 40 minutes or until browned on all sides and cooked through.

SERVES 6
APPROXIMATELY 7.1 GRAMS FAT PER SERVING

◆ ◆ ◆ ◆ ◆

THAI BEEF SALAD

▶ ▶

L̲ean flank steak and a blend of lime juice and mint give this salad its distinctive taste. It is best served at room temperature or slightly chilled.

³/₄ pound flank steak, in one piece, trimmed of all
     visible fat
     Vegetable oil cooking spray
1   small red onion, coarsely chopped
1   clove garlic, finely minced
1   teaspoon ground ginger
1   tablespoon crushed dried mint
¹/₄ teaspoon hot red pepper flakes (optional)
1   teaspoon sugar (optional)
1   medium cucumber, peeled, seeded, and diced
3   ripe plum tomatoes, seeded and diced
     Salt and freshly ground pepper to taste
¹/₄ cup fresh lime juice
2   teaspoons low sodium soy sauce
2   scallions, white and tender greens, finely sliced
     Large lettuce leaves
2   tablespoons chopped fresh mint or cilantro
     Lemon or lime wedges for garnish

1. Preheat broiler.

2. Place flank steak on a broiler pan, coat steak lightly with cooking spray, and broil about 4 inches from heat for 4 minutes per side for medium rare, or to desired degree of doneness. Remove from oven and place on a platter to cool.

3. Heat a nonstick skillet coated with cooking spray. Add onion to skillet and cook over medium-low heat, stirring, for 2 minutes. Add garlic, ginger, dried mint, hot pepper flakes and sugar if desired, and cook for an additional 2 minutes. Transfer contents of skillet to a large mixing bowl and cool to room temperature.

4. When beef has cooled, cut against the grain into very thin slices and add to onion mixture in bowl. Add cucumber and tomatoes and toss lightly. Taste and add salt and pepper, if desired. Add lime juice, soy sauce, and scallions and toss again until ingredients are well combined.

5. Arrange lettuce leaves on individual serving dishes. Spoon equal amounts of beef mixture over lettuce and sprinkle with chopped mint or cilantro. Serve garnished with lemon or lime wedges.

SERVES 4
APPROXIMATELY 9.3 GRAMS FAT PER SERVING

♦ ♦ ♦ ♦ ♦

VEAL CHOPS
WITH MUSHROOMS AND SAGE

▶ ▶

The leaves of the sage plant enjoy a long-standing and intimate relationship with veal cooked in white wine. And after trying in vain to grow my own, I now buy them in branches from a local Italian market and keep them stored in tightly closed glass jars in my cool (if crowded) cupboard. If you can't find fresh sage, dried whole leaves are satisfactory.

A pasta or potato dish goes well with the veal.

> Olive oil cooking spray
> 1   teaspoon olive oil
> 4   loin veal chops (about 7 ounces each with bone
>   and fat), trimmed of all visible fat
> 2   cloves garlic, chopped, or to taste
> 1½ cups cleaned, thinly sliced mushrooms
> ¼   cup Low Fat Chicken Broth (page 43) or canned
>   low-sodium broth
> 4   large fresh sage leaves or ¼ teaspoon crumbled
>   dried leaves
> ½   cup dry white wine
>   Salt and freshly ground pepper to taste

1. Coat a large nonstick skillet with cooking spray, add oil and heat. Add veal chops and sauté quickly over medium-high heat for about 2 minutes or until lightly golden. Turn and sauté other side until golden. Transfer chops to a platter and keep warm.

2. Lower heat and, if necessary, add a little more cooking spray to skillet (remove skillet from flame to do this) and add garlic and mushrooms. Cook just until garlic begins to color, add broth, and cook until mushrooms are tender and liquid has evaporated. Remove mushrooms from pan with a slotted spoon, raise heat, add sage and wine, and cook until liquid is reduced by half.

3. Return veal to hot skillet and cook for about 2 minutes per side, add mushrooms and heat through. Sprinkle with salt and pepper, if desired, and serve immediately.

SERVES 4
APPROXIMATELY 7.0 GRAMS FAT PER SERVING

◆ ◆ ◆ ◆

VEAL STEW WITH SWEET PEAS

▶ ▶

I created this dish one evening when I craved a plate of *osso buco*, a tasty northern Italian dish traditionally prepared with meaty (and fatty) veal shanks. By substituting a leaner cut of veal and reducing the portions a little, I can satisfy my craving almost anytime.

Simple risotto and a salad of Boston lettuce with lemon juice and a dash of olive oil work well with this robust stew.

	Vegetable oil cooking spray
1	teaspoon vegetable oil
3/4	pound lean veal shoulder, trimmed of all visible fat and cut into 1-inch cubes
1/2	cup chopped onion
1	large clove garlic, minced
3/4	cup sliced carrots
3/4	cup sliced celery
1/2	cup clean, sliced mushrooms
3	ounces lean (95% fat free) cooked ham, thinly sliced and cut in pieces
1	teaspoon tomato paste (preferably sun-dried)
1	tablespoon flour
1	cup canned no-salt-added chopped tomatoes, undrained
1/2	teaspoon dried thyme
1	large bay leaf
3/4	cup dry white wine
1	cup low sodium beef broth

Salt and freshly ground pepper to taste
1   *cup green peas, fresh or frozen and thawed*
1/4   *cup chopped fresh parsley*

1. Preheat oven to 350°F.

2. Coat a large ovenproof pot or casserole with cooking spray, add oil, and heat. Add veal, a few cubes at a time, and cook over medium-high heat until brown on all sides. Don't crowd the meat or it won't brown properly. Transfer veal to a plate as it is browned and keep warm.

3. Lower heat to medium, add onion, garlic, carrots, celery, and mushrooms and cook for 7 or 8 minutes or until vegetables are soft. Add ham and cook, stirring occasionally, for another 2 minutes.

4. Add tomato paste and flour and stir over low heat until well blended. Return veal to pot, add tomatoes, thyme, bay leaf, wine, and broth (add additional wine or water, if necessary, to cover the veal completely with liquid). Taste and add salt and pepper, if desired. Raise heat and bring to a boil.

5. Cover and place in preheated oven for 1 1/4 hours. Add peas and cook for an additional 15 minutes. Alternatively, you can cook the stew on top of the stove for about the same length of time over a very low flame. Either way, check occasionally and add wine or water, if necessary. Stew is done when the veal is fork tender. Taste and adjust seasonings, if necessary, and stir in parsley just before serving.

SERVES 4

APPROXIMATELY 5.8 GRAMS FAT PER SERVING

◆ ◆ ◆ ◆ ◆

SKEWERED SPICED LAMB

▶ ▶

Over the years I have dined at numerous Indian restaurants and while I haven't fully dealt with all the intricacies and subtle nuances of that country's cooking, I do enjoy preparing skewered kebabs with my own assortment of traditional Indian spices.

The preparation and skewering of the kebabs can be done in no time at all. The cooking time for the kebabs is only about ten minutes when cooked under a broiler.

The classic accompaniment for this dish is plain rice, but try it with couscous or an uncomplicated bulgur salad for a nice change of texture and taste.

1	*pound lean lamb, preferably from the leg, trimmed of all visible fat*
1	*small onion, grated or finely minced*
3	*cloves garlic, crushed*
1	*teaspoon freshly grated ginger root*
1	*tablespoon finely minced fresh parsley*
2	*tablespoons red wine vinegar*
1	*teaspoon hot chili powder, or to taste*
$^1/_2$	*teaspoon ground cinnamon*
$^1/_4$	*cup low sodium beef broth*
	Salt and freshly ground pepper to taste

1. Cut lamb into 1½-inch cubes and transfer to a mixing bowl.

2. Combine remaining ingredients and stir until thoroughly blended. Pour mixture over lamb, cover and marinate

for at least 2 hours at room temperature or refrigerate over-night. Stir or turn meat occasionally.

3. Prepare grill or preheat broiler.

4. Reserving marinade, remove lamb and thread cubes on long metal skewers. Cook 4 inches from heat, turning often and basting occasionally with marinade, for 8 to 10 minutes depending on desired degree of doneness. Serve immediately.

SERVES 4

APPROXIMATELY 5.3 GRAMS FAT PER SERVING

♦ ♦ ♦ ♦ ♦

BRAISED LAMB AND LEEKS

▶ ▶

In this dish I combine the leanest lamb with my beloved leeks and braise them with wine, broth, and vegetables. The resulting taste is sensational and needs only a simple salad to complete the feast.

Vegetable oil cooking spray

3/4 *pound lean lamb, preferably from the leg, trimmed of all visible fat and cut into 1-inch cubes*

3 *leeks, white and tender greens, well rinsed and drained*

1 *small onion, chopped*

1/2 *cup dry white wine*

2 *cups Low Fat Chicken Broth (page 43) or canned low-sodium broth*

2 *cups water*

2 *teaspoons Worcestershire sauce*

1 *teaspoon dried thyme*

1 *bay leaf*

1 *tablespoon chopped fresh parsley or 1/2 tablespoon dried*

Salt and freshly ground pepper to taste

1 *medium red bell pepper, cored, seeded, and cut into thin strips*

1 *medium potato, peeled and thinly sliced*

Parsley sprigs for garnish

1. Coat a large nonstick skillet with cooking spray. Add lamb and cook over medium heat, stirring occasionally, until browned.

---

2. Cut leeks crosswise into 1-inch slices and add to skillet. Add remaining ingredients, except bell pepper and potato, and bring mixture to a boil. Reduce heat to very low, cover, and simmer gently for 30 minutes.

3. Add red pepper and potato, cover, and simmer for an additional 10 minutes or until potato is tender. Remove cover, raise heat, and cook for 5 minutes or until liquid is reduced by about half. Taste and correct seasonings if necessary.

4. Transfer to a heated platter, garnish with parsley sprigs, and serve.

SERVES 4

APPROXIMATELY 6.2 GRAMS FAT PER SERVING

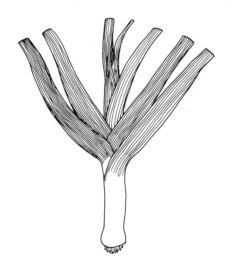

◆ ◆ ◆ ◆ ◆

STUFFED PORK TENDERLOIN

▶▶▶▶▶▶▶▶▶▶▶▶▶▶▶▶▶▶▶▶▶▶▶▶▶▶

Although tenderloin is one of the most expensive cuts of pork, it is also the most tender and the leanest. My fat-wise recipe calls for flattening the meat, stuffing it, rolling it, and slow roasting it. The results are succulent and rich with flavor.

For a flamboyant presentation, you might offer a side dish of apple rings broiled with lemon juice and a sprinkling of sugar, Baked Potato "Puffs" (page 172), and Wilted Spinach with Tangy Sauce (page 182).

$^1/_2$	ounce dried porcini mushrooms
$^3/_4$	cup hot water
	Vegetable oil cooking spray
2	teaspoons vegetable oil
1	cup chopped onions
$^3/_4$	cup pimientos, coarsely chopped
$1^1/_4$	pounds pork tenderloin, trimmed of all visible fat
2	large cloves garlic, minced
2	teaspoons dried rosemary, crushed
	Salt and freshly ground pepper to taste

1. Soak porcini mushrooms in hot water for 45 minutes.

2. Preheat oven to 375°F. Lightly coat a roasting pan with cooking spray and set aside.

3. Heat oil in large nonstick skillet. Add onions and cook over medium-low heat, stirring occasionally, for 5 minutes. Raise heat slightly and sauté until onions begin to brown.

4. Drain mushrooms, squeezing out as much liquid as possible, and coarsely chop. Discard liquid, add mushrooms to skillet, and stir in pimientos. Cook for 2 minutes then turn off heat.

5. Cut tenderloin down the center lengthwise to within 1/2 inch of the bottom. Spread open, place between two sheets of wax paper, and pound to a thickness of about 1/2 inch.

6. Rub exposed side of pork with garlic and rosemary, salt to taste, sprinkle liberally with pepper, and spread mushroom-onion mixture on top. Roll roast, and tie (not too tightly) at 2-inch intervals with kitchen string.

7. Place roast, seam side down, in prepared roasting pan, spray top of roast lightly with cooking oil, and roast for 1 hour.

8. Remove roast from oven and let sit, draped loosely in foil, for 5 minutes. Cut away string, cut tenderloin into 1/2-inch slices and serve immediately.

SERVES 4

APPROXIMATELY 4.2 GRAMS FAT PER SERVING

PORK SOUVLAKI

The pork in these Greek lunchtime favorites serves as a flavoring factor rather than the main ingredient. It enters the pita pockets along with lettuce, tomatoes, onions, and a delightful blend of garlic-kissed yogurt—a complete meal in a sandwich.

2 medium cloves garlic, pressed
1/2 teaspoon each dried oregano, thyme, and rosemary
1/4 cup red wine vinegar
1 teaspoon olive oil
3/4 pound pork tenderloin, trimmed of all visible fat and cut into 1 1/2-inch cubes
1 1/2 cups low fat plain yogurt
   Salt and freshly ground pepper to taste
4 large pitas (preferably whole wheat)
2 large, ripe tomatoes, each cut into 8 wedges
2 cups shredded romaine lettuce
1/2 medium red onion, thinly sliced

1. Combine 1 clove garlic, herbs, vinegar, and oil.

2. Place pork cubes into a shallow baking dish, pour vinegar mixture over, and refrigerate covered, for at least 2 hours. Turn pork occasionally in marinade.

3. Combine yogurt and remaining garlic and set aside.

4. Prepare grill or preheat broiler.

5. Reserving marinade, remove pork and thread onto long metal skewers. Broil or grill pork about 5 inches from

heat source, turning often and basting with marinade, for 10 to 12 minutes or until cooked through but not dry. Sprinkle with salt and pepper, if desired.

6. Cut pitas to make two half pockets each and heat briefly in oven.

7. Divide pork, tomatoes, lettuce, onion slices, and yogurt mixture evenly among pita halves and serve, two halves per person.

SERVES 4
APPROXIMATELY 4.5 GRAMS FAT PER SERVING

POULTRY

◆ ◆ ◆ ◆ ◆

CURRIED CHICKEN

▶ ▶

If it's true that every good story needs a hero, one of the saviors of the many bibles of low fat cooking is chicken. In this mouth-watering dish, chicken pieces are simmered in broth, vinegar, and vegetables. After removing the chicken, tomatoes, apricots, ginger, curry powder, and flour-thickened sour cream are added for a brief but thorough comingling. Low fat? You bet! But this curried chicken is so rich-tasting it rates a perfect 10 for healthy good taste.

Serve with Spinach Raita (page 22) and plain steamed rice to help soak up every drop of the sauce.

2¹/₂	pounds chicken, skinned, trimmed of all visible fat and cut into serving pieces
2	cups Low Fat Chicken Broth (page 43) or canned low sodium broth
2	tablespoons red wine vinegar
1	carrot, thinly sliced
1	medium onion, thinly sliced
1	clove garlic, minced
2	tablespoons no-salt-added tomato paste
2	ripe tomatoes, chopped
4	dried apricot halves, diced
1	teaspoon freshly grated ginger root or ¹/₂ teaspoon powdered
1	tablespoon hot or mild curry powder, or to taste
	Salt and freshly ground pepper to taste
1	tablespoon flour

2   tablespoons light sour cream
       Parsley sprigs for garnish

1. Rinse chicken and pat dry.

2. Combine broth and vinegar in a large, deep skillet. Add carrot, onion, and garlic, and cook over low heat until simmering. Add chicken, cover, and simmer over low heat for about 40 minutes or until chicken is cooked through, turning pieces halfway through cooking time. Remove chicken from skillet and keep warm.

3. Add tomato paste to skillet and stir until well blended. Add tomatoes, apricots, ginger, curry powder, and salt and pepper to taste. Cook over medium heat, stirring constantly, for 1 minute. Cover and simmer gently for 5 minutes.

4. Blend flour with sour cream and stir into skillet. Cook over very low heat, stirring often, for 2 minutes or until ingredients are thoroughly blended and sauce thickens. Taste and correct seasonings, if necessary.

5. Arrange chicken on a heated serving platter and spoon on half the sauce from the skillet. Garnish with parsley sprigs and serve remaining sauce on the side.

SERVES 4
APPROXIMATELY 6.8 GRAMS FAT PER SERVING

◆ ◆ ◆ ◆ ◆

CHICKEN BAKED IN YOGURT

▶ ▶

Cooks from the Mideast, Russia, and India, among others, have long benefited from marinating chicken in plain or seasoned yogurt. It makes the meat more succulent and allows the flavor of the blended spices to develop and seep deep within.

Serve with noodles or rice, accompanied with roasted sweet peppers or crisp-steamed green beans.

2   whole chicken breasts with bone (*about 2 pounds*), *skinned, halved, and trimmed of all visible fat*
1   *cup low fat plain yogurt*
2   *cloves garlic, pressed*
2   *teaspoons dried tarragon*
    Salt and freshly ground pepper to taste
2   *teaspoons olive oil*
1   *small onion, thinly sliced*
3/4 *cup clean, thinly sliced mushrooms*
2   *teaspoons cornstarch*
1/4 *cup water or dry white wine*

1. Preheat oven to 350°F.

2. Rinse chicken, pat dry, and place in a large, shallow dish.

3. Blend yogurt with garlic, tarragon, and salt and pepper. Spoon mixture over chicken. Cover and marinate at room temperature for 15 minutes, turning once.

4. Meanwhile, heat oil in a nonstick skillet. Add onion

and mushrooms and cook over medium-high heat, stirring, for 2 minutes. Dissolve cornstarch in water or wine and add to skillet with onion and mushrooms. Stir until thickened.

5. Reserving marinade, transfer chicken to a shallow baking dish or ovenproof casserole.

6. Add contents of skillet to marinade and stir until all ingredients are thoroughly blended. Pour mixture over chicken. Cover and bake for 20 minutes. Uncover and bake for an additional 15 minutes.

SERVES 4

APPROXIMATELY 5.0 GRAMS FAT PER SERVING

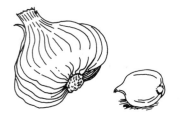

GINGER ORANGE CHICKEN

▶ ▶

In addition to being one of the least expensive basic foods, chicken is versatile, quick, and easy to prepare. One of my favorite chicken dishes is this unusual creation. Crunchy outside, tender and smartly spiced inside, serve it with crisp steamed broccoli or cauliflower dressed with a sprinkling of fresh lemon juice.

> 1 *pound boneless, skinless chicken breasts, halved and trimmed of all visible fat*
> 1 *tablespoon honey*
> 1 *tablespoon Worcestershire sauce*
> 1 *teaspoon freshly grated ginger root or* $1/2$ *teaspoon powdered*
> $1/4$ *teaspoon hot paprika*
> $1/2$ *cup orange juice*
> 1 *tablespoon olive oil*
> *Salt and freshly ground pepper to taste*
> $1/2$ *cup wheat germ*
> *Vegetable oil cooking spray*

1. Rinse chicken, pat dry, and place in a large, shallow bowl.

2. Combine honey, Worcestershire, ginger, paprika, orange juice, and oil, whisking well. Brush mixture over chicken and marinate, refrigerated, for at least 1 hour, turning once or twice.

3. Preheat oven to 350°F.

4. Remove chicken from bowl, sprinkle lightly with salt

and pepper if desired, and coat with wheat germ. Place chicken breasts on a baking sheet coated lightly with cooking spray and roast for 35 minutes or until golden and cooked through.

SERVES **4**
APPROXIMATELY **6.8** GRAMS FAT PER SERVING

◆ ◆ ◆ ◆ ◆

CHICKEN EGGPLANT KABOB

▶ ▶

𝕮all it shish kabob, brochette, or shashlik, the technique for cooking skewered food is simple. In preparing this dish, mixing the tasty marinade and threading the skewers are the most energetic tasks you'll face (with the possible exception of giving out copies of the recipe).

An excellent accompaniment is the Risotto Milanese (page 157). Start the risotto before you skewer the chicken and place the kebabs on the grill or under the broiler as the rice cooks. This way, the dishes will be ready for presentation at the same time.

1	pound boneless, skinless chicken breasts, trimmed of all visible fat
1/2	cup white wine vinegar
2	teaspoons olive oil
1	teaspoon dried crumbled rosemary, or to taste
4	cloves garlic, pressed
	Juice of 2 large lemons
1	small eggplant (about 3/4 pound), unpeeled
16	cherry tomatoes
8	small white boiling onions
	Salt and freshly ground pepper to taste

1. Rinse chicken, pat dry, and cut into 1-inch cubes.

2. Combine vinegar, oil, rosemary, garlic, and the juice of 1 lemon. Toss chicken in marinade in a shallow baking dish, cover, and refrigerate for at least 2 hours. Stir mixture once or twice during that time.

3. Prepare grill or preheat broiler.

4. While grill or broiler heats, cut eggplant into 1-inch cubes and toss with the juice of the remaining lemon.

5. Thread long metal skewers, alternating chicken, eggplant, cherry tomatoes, and onions. Reserve marinade.

6. Broil or grill for about 7 minutes, turning and brushing occasionally with reserved marinade. Sprinkle with salt and pepper, if desired.

SERVES 4
APPROXIMATELY 4.2 GRAMS FAT PER SERVING

BAKED CHICKEN
WITH SAUCE DIABLE

▶ ▶

To corrupt a phrase: spice delivers variety to life—or, in this case, to chicken. Baked and presented with a sauce boat of Sauce Diable, the results are nothing less than divine!

Serve with steamed zucchini rounds drizzled with lemon juice and a touch of olive oil, fresh-off-the-cob corn with pimientos, and a cold vegetable salad (perhaps a combination of steamed broccoli, cauliflower, green beans, tomatoes, carrots, or whatever) with Oil-Free Herb Vinaigrette (page 10).

$2^1/_2$ *pounds chicken, skinned, trimmed of all visible fat, and cut into serving pieces*
$^1/_4$ *cup orange juice*
  Hot red pepper sauce to taste
$^1/_2$ *cup fine dry bread crumbs*
1 *teaspoon olive oil*
1 *large shallot, minced*
2 *cloves garlic, minced*
$^1/_2$ *cup dry white wine*
2 *tablespoons red wine vinegar*
$^1/_2$ *cup tomato ketchup (low sodium if desired)*
1 *teaspoon Worcestershire sauce*
2 *tablespoons chopped fresh parsley*

1. Rinse chicken and pat dry. Place chicken in a bowl and add orange juice blended with a dash of hot pepper

sauce. Stir to cover all surfaces of chicken and marinate for 15 minutes.

2. Remove chicken from marinade and coat with bread crumbs, pressing crumbs well onto all sides. Refrigerate chicken for 30 minutes.

3. Preheat oven to 350°F.

4. Place chicken in a shallow baking pan and bake for 30 minutes or until cooked through and golden.

5. While chicken bakes, heat oil in a nonstick skillet and sauté shallot and garlic over medium-low heat until translucent. Raise heat, add wine and vinegar and cook to reduce slightly, about 3 minutes. Add ketchup, Worcestershire, another dash of hot pepper sauce, and parsley, and simmer for 10 minutes.

6. Arrange baked chicken on a platter and serve sauce separately.

SERVES 4

APPROXIMATELY 7.5 GRAMS FAT PER SERVING

◆ ◆ ◆ ◆ ◆

CHICKEN FAJITAS

▶ ▶

These south-of-the-border specialties are fun to eat. Serve them surrounded by coarsely shredded romaine lettuce and tomato wedges, with a dollop of light sour cream (1 gram fat per tablespoon), and/or a mild salsa.

1	*pound boneless, skinless chicken breasts, trimmed of all visible fat*
¹/₄	*cup dry red wine*
2	*sun-dried tomato halves (not oil-packed), chopped*
1	*medium clove garlic, chopped*
¹/₄	*cup fresh lime juice*
1	*tablespoon fresh lemon juice*
1	*tablespoon red wine vinegar*
2	*teaspoons olive oil*
¹/₄	*teaspoon ground cumin*
	Vegetable oil cooking spray
1	*medium red onion, halved lengthwise and thinly sliced*
1	*large green pepper, seeded and cut into thin strips*
1	*small jalapeño pepper, fresh or canned and drained, seeded and chopped (wear rubber gloves)*
8	*flour tortillas*

1. Rinse chicken, pat dry, and set aside.

2. Combine wine and sun-dried tomato halves in a small saucepan and heat just to simmering. Remove from heat and set aside to cool.

3. In a bowl, combine garlic, lime juice, lemon juice,

Poultry ◆ **97**

vinegar, oil, cumin, and tomatoes with their cooled soaking liquid. Whisk or stir well to blend. Reserve 3 tablespoons of marinade, transfer remainder to a shallow baking dish, and add chicken, turning to coat. Cover and refrigerate for at least 1 hour, turning occasionally.

4. Preheat broiler.

5. Broil chicken pieces, turning occasionally and brushing with marinade from the baking dish, for about 10 minutes per side or until cooked through.

6. While chicken cooks, heat a nonstick skillet coated with cooking spray and sauté onion, bell pepper, and jalapeño over medium heat until wilted. If skillet is very dry, add 1 tablespoon of reserved marinade. When vegetables are wilted, add remaining 2 tablespoons marinade and cook until onion is very soft.

7. Remove chicken from oven and turn oven off. Slice chicken into ¼-inch strips and toss briefly with mixture in skillet. Cover and keep warm for a few moments. Meanwhile, place tortillas on ovenproof plates and place in oven for 2 or 3 minutes or until tortillas are just warmed. Remove, divide filling among tortillas, roll, and serve two to a plate.

SERVES 4
APPROXIMATELY 9.8 GRAMS FAT PER SERVING

◆ ◆ ◆ ◆ ◆

HERBED CHICKEN SALAD

▶ ▶

A refreshing salad for a hot summer day or evening. This chicken salad also makes lovely luncheon sandwiches when packed in whole-wheat pita pockets with fresh ripe tomatoes, and travels well to the office, terrace or patio, picnic grounds, beach, or ball game.

$1/2$	cup low fat plain yogurt
1	tablespoon light sour cream
3	scallions, white and tender greens, finely chopped
1	small clove garlic, minced (optional)
2	teaspoons chopped fresh dillweed or 1 teaspoon dried
1	teaspoon finely chopped fresh thyme or $1/2$ teaspoon dried
1	pound boneless, skinless chicken breasts, trimmed of all visible fat
$1/2$	cup dry white wine
$1/2$	cup water
4	whole peppercorns
$1/2$	medium onion, sliced
$1/2$	medium cucumber, peeled, seeded, and cubed
1	teaspoon lemon juice
	Salt and freshly ground pepper to taste
4	medium radicchio leaves, rinsed
8	medium bibb lettuce leaves, rinsed and dried
8	ripe cherry tomatoes
4	sprigs fresh dillweed

1. Combine yogurt, sour cream, scallions, garlic, chopped dill, and thyme in a medium bowl. Refrigerate for 1 hour to blend flavors.

2. Combine chicken, wine, water, peppercorns, and onion in a deep skillet or saucepan and bring to a boil. Reduce heat, cover, and poach chicken for 15 minutes. Remove from heat and allow chicken to cool in its poaching liquid. Drain, discard liquid, and chill chicken completely.

3. Cut chilled chicken into bite-size cubes and add to yogurt sauce, stirring gently.

4. Add fresh cucumber and lemon juice and taste, adding salt and pepper if desired.

5. Serve on a bed of radicchio and bibb lettuce garnished with cherry tomatoes and dill sprigs.

SERVES 4

APPROXIMATELY 3.0 GRAMS FAT PER SERVING

♦ ♦ ♦ ♦ ♦

TURKEY SCALLOPS
IN SHERRY ROSEMARY SAUCE

▶ ▶

This is one of the tastiest and easiest ways of preparing turkey scallops. You should have the dish on the table in less than 30 minutes.

If you like pasta, choose your favorite kind and toss it with **Thick and Rich Tomato Sauce** (page 3) combined with any leftover sauce from the turkey. Serve with sautéed string beans, steamed carrots, and zucchini rounds.

> 1   *pound turkey breast tenderloins, cut into ¹/₂-inch thick slices*
> 2   *tablespoons flour, preferably superfine*
> 2   *teaspoons vegetable oil*
> 2   *tablespoons medium-dry sherry*
> 2   *medium shallots, minced*
> 2   *teaspoons dried rosemary, crushed*
> 1   *cup Low Fat Chicken Broth (page 43) or canned low-sodium broth*
>   *Salt and freshly ground pepper to taste*
> 1   *tablespoon fresh lemon juice*

1. Dredge turkey in flour and shake off excess.

2. Heat oil in a nonstick skillet. Add turkey and cook over medium heat, shaking pan often, for about 5 minutes on each side or until lightly golden. Remove turkey from pan and keep warm.

3. Add sherry, shallots, and rosemary to skillet, reduce heat slightly and cook, stirring often, for 2 minutes. Raise

heat to medium-high, pour in broth, and cook, stirring, until liquid is reduced by half. Season to taste with salt and pepper, and swirl in lemon juice.

4. Return turkey to pan just briefly to coat with sauce, arrange on a heated platter or among individual warmed plates, top with sauce, and serve.

SERVES 4
APPROXIMATELY 4.8 GRAMS FAT PER SERVING

◆ ◆ ◆ ◆ ◆

TURKEY-STUFFED CABBAGE ROLLS

▶ ▶

I'm just crazy for cabbage. I like it in all forms: in soup, raw in salads and slaws, braised, steamed, stir-fried, and above all, stuffed!

Here is my low fat version of the classic dish, substituting tasty ground turkey for the red meat. You lose nothing in the translation save saturated fat. Green or red cabbage works equally well, but red cabbage gives the dish a rich mahogany color.

There's little rice in this dish, so plain cooked rice is a perfect adjunct, ideal for soaking up the rich fruity sauce. Or try it over a bed of fresh spinach leaves steamed with a touch of garlic.

1	medium head green or red cabbage, about 1³/₄ pounds
³/₄	pound lean ground turkey
¹/₂	cup uncooked rice
1	medium onion, grated
1	medium carrot, grated
1	egg
	Salt and freshly ground pepper to taste
1	large apple, preferably Granny Smith, cored, peeled, and coarsely chopped
¹/₂	cup golden raisins
1	cup dry red wine
2	cups low sodium tomato sauce

1   cup water, approximately
1¹/₂   tablespoons fresh lemon juice

1. Core cabbage and place in a large pot with enough water to nearly cover. Cover, bring to a boil, and cook for about 5 minutes or until leaves are soft. Drain well. Carefully remove the outer 12 leaves and set aside. Dice remaining cabbage and set aside.

2. Combine turkey with rice, onion, carrot, egg, and salt and pepper. Mix until ingredients are thoroughly blended.

3. Separate turkey mixture into 12 balls and place a ball in center of each cabbage leaf. Roll up each leaf, tucking ends in securely after the first roll.

4. In a large pot, place rolls close together, seam-side down, stacking rolls if necessary. Add diced cabbage, apple, and raisins to pot.

5. Combine wine, tomato sauce, water, and lemon juice and pour over cabbage rolls in pot, adding additional water to cover rolls if necessary. Bring to a boil, then reduce heat to low, cover and simmer for about 1 hour.

SERVES 4

APPROXIMATELY 8.0 GRAMS FAT PER SERVING

♦ ♦ ♦ ♦ ♦

TURKEY ROULADES

▶ ▶

R*oulade* is the French term for a thin slice of meat, or in this case, poultry, rolled around a filling such as the one I've suggested here. The rolled-up package is secured with string or a toothpick, browned and then braised in a cooking liquid.

This is the kind of dish guests will think you fussed over forever—so don't tell them otherwise. Simple parslied red-skinned potatoes and a steamed green vegetable make worthy companions.

> 8   turkey breast cutlets (*about 1¼ pounds*)
>   Vegetable oil cooking spray (*preferably olive oil*)
> 2   large shallots, chopped
> 1   large clove garlic, minced
> ¾   cup Low Fat Chicken Broth (*page 43*) or canned
>   low-sodium broth
> 2   tablespoons chopped fresh parsley
> 1   ounce very lean ham (*95% fat free*), cut in small
>   pieces
>   Salt and freshly ground pepper to taste
> ½   cup dry white wine

1. Rinse turkey, pat dry, and pound very thin between sheets of wax paper. Set aside.

2. Coat a nonstick skillet with cooking spray and sauté shallots and garlic over medium-low heat, stirring often, until the shallots begin to brown. Add 2 tablespoons broth and

cook until the broth is nearly evaporated. Remove from heat and stir in parsley and ham.

3. Divide filling among the cutlets, spreading with a spatula, and roll cutlets firmly, securing each with a toothpick. Sprinkle with salt and pepper, if desired.

4. Add a little additional cooking spray to the skillet, if necessary, and brown the turkey rolls over medium heat, turning as the sides become golden.

5. When the turkey is browned, remove from pan, turn the heat up to medium-high and pour in the wine and remaining broth, stirring to loosen any browned bits. Cook for about 2 minutes.

6. Lower heat and return the roulades to the pan, cover lightly and cook for about 5 minutes or until the turkey is cooked through. Transfer the roulades to heated plates, remove toothpicks, pour the juices over them, and serve.

SERVES 4

APPROXIMATELY 6.0 GRAMS FAT PER SERVING

◆ ◆ ◆ ◆ ◆

ROAST TURKEY AND YAMS
WITH CITRUS CURRANT SAUCE

▶ ▶

Festive enough for a holiday meal, this delicious dish is so rich in nutrients and low in fat it's a welcome treat anytime at all. The piquant citrus and red current sauce can be prepared in advance and refrigerated for up to one month. For a hearty dinner, start with my Acorn Squash and Apple Soup (page 59).

1	large orange
1/2	large lemon
1	cup red currant jelly
1	tablespoon red wine vinegar
2	tablespoons port wine
2	tablespoons Marsala or cream sherry
2	teaspoons sugar
1 1/2	teaspoons Dijon mustard
	Pinch cayenne
	Vegetable oil cooking spray
1 1/2	pounds boneless, skinless turkey breast, in one piece (thawed if frozen)
6	medium sweet potatoes, cut crosswise into 1 1/4-inch slices
	Salt and freshly ground pepper to taste.

1. Juice orange and lemon and set juice aside. Peel orange and lemon, taking care not to include any of the bitter white pith. Cut the peels into julienne strips (matchstick size) and simmer in 1/4 cup water for 10 minutes. Drain.

2. Combine reserved juices and cooked peels in a saucepan. Add currant jelly, vinegar, port wine, Marsala or sherry, sugar, mustard, and cayenne, and bring to a boil. Reduce heat immediately and simmer gently over very low heat for about 45 minutes.

3. Preheat oven to 350°F.

4. Place turkey breast in center of a large shallow roasting pan coated with cooking spray. Surround turkey with sweet potato slices. Spray turkey and sweet potatoes lightly with cooking oil and sprinkle with salt and pepper. Spoon about ¼ cup of sauce over turkey and potatoes and roast for about 40 minutes, or until a meat thermometer inserted in thickest part of breast registers 180°F. Reserving ½ cup of sauce, baste turkey every 10 minutes with remaining sauce.

5. Remove roasting pan from oven and let stand for 5 minutes. Transfer turkey to a cutting board and cut into thin slices. Arrange slices on a heated serving platter and surround with potatoes.

6. Place roasting pan on stovetop over medium-high heat, stir in remaining ½ cup of sauce, and cook until well heated, stirring constantly. Spoon sauce from roasting pan over turkey and potatoes and serve.

SERVES 6

APPROXIMATELY 2.2 GRAMS FAT PER SERVING

FISH
and
SHELLFISH

♦ ♦ ♦ ♦ ♦

MAHIMAHI IN GRAPE SAUCE

▶ ▶

Mahimahi, also known as dolphin fish (not to be confused with the mammal dolphin or porpoise), has been appearing on more and more restaurant menus, which is fortunate since it is delicious and very low in calories and fat. Here, the fish is poached and served with a sauce made with fresh grapes, my low-fat adaptation of the rich French *Véronique* sauce.

1/2	small onion, sliced
1	clove garlic, quartered
1	tablespoon fresh lemon juice
6	whole peppercorns
1/4	teaspoon each: dried thyme, rosemary, and parsley
1	bay leaf
1	cup dry white wine
1/2	cup water
1 1/4	pounds mahimahi fillets
1	tablespoon unsalted diet margarine
1	tablespoon flour
1/4	cup half-and-half
	Salt and freshly ground pepper to taste
2	cups fresh seedless green grapes

1. In a large, deep skillet, combine onion, garlic, lemon juice, peppercorns, herbs, wine, and water. Bring to a boil, then reduce heat and simmer gently for 5 minutes.

2. Add fish to skillet. Cover, and simmer over very low heat for 10 minutes or until fish is cooked through. Carefully

remove fish from skillet, arrange fillets on a heated serving platter and keep warm. Strain and reserve liquid from skillet, discarding solids.

3. Melt margarine in skillet. Remove from heat, add flour and 2 tablespoons reserved cooking liquid and stir until smooth. Return to heat, add remaining cooking liquid and half-and-half, and cook over low heat, stirring constantly, until mixture thickens. Season with salt and pepper, add grapes, and cook until heated through.

4. Pour sauce over fish and serve.

SERVES 4
APPROXIMATELY 6.2 GRAMS FAT PER SERVING

◆ ◆ ◆ ◆

OVEN-STEAMED RED SNAPPER
IN PARCHMENT

▶ ▶

$\mathbb{C}$ooked in a parchment envelope, the ingredients in this dish steam and bake at the same time, the gentle aroma of the fish, herbs, and spices billowing out as the envelopes are opened at the dinner table.

If baking parchment is unavailable, aluminum foil makes an acceptable, if less dramatic, substitute. And any low fat fish fillet—cod, sole, flounder—can be substituted for the snapper.

> 4 *sheets baking parchment, approximately 10 inches by 12 inches each*
> *Olive oil cooking spray*
> 1 *pound red snapper fillets, divided into four equal portions*
> 1 *small white onion, thinly sliced*
> 1¼ *cups chopped plum tomatoes, fresh or no-salt-added canned, and drained*
> 4 *large fresh basil leaves, slivered*
> *Pinch hot red pepper flakes, or to taste*
> *Salt and freshly ground pepper to taste*

1. Preheat oven to 400°F.

2. Trim each piece of parchment into an oval shape and fold crosswise in half. Spray the center of the bottom half of each oval with olive oil.

3. Lay a fish fillet over the oil, sprinkle with ¼ of the onion slices, spoon on ¼ of the chopped tomatoes, sprinkle

with basil shreds, hot pepper flakes if desired, and salt and pepper to taste. Fold the top half of the parchment over fish, fold edges over twice to enclose fish completely (but loosely, as the parchment will puff up as it cooks) and flatten the fold firmly with the side of a heavy knife. Repeat with remaining parchment and fish fillets.

4. Place parchment envelopes on large, ungreased baking sheets and bake 6 minutes for thin fillets or 8 minutes if they are thick.

5. Cut open the top of the parchment along the fold, turn it back (be careful of the steam), and serve immediately.

SERVES 4

APPROXIMATELY 2.0 GRAMS FAT PER SERVING

GRILLED TUNA
WITH BLACK PEPPERCORN SAUCE

▶ ▶

Fish cooked on the grill or under the broiler should have a soft resistance when it is done. Although tuna, like sword-fish, benefits from the higher temperatures of a grill, the fire should not be so hot that the flesh sizzles and blackens. Ideally, grill marks should be golden in color.

I've discovered that the easiest and neatest way to crush peppercorns is to put them in a sturdy envelope and roll over the envelope with a bottle or rolling pin, or smash it with a skillet.

Cool down this peppery dish with cooked potatoes tossed with Creamy Shallot Dressing (page 12).

1	tablespoon coarsely crushed black peppercorns, or to taste
2	tablespoons Worcestershire sauce
2	tablespoons fresh lemon juice
2	teaspoons olive oil
4	yellowfin tuna steaks (about 1¼ pounds)
¼	cup Low Fat Chicken Broth (page 43) or canned low-sodium broth
¼	cup dry white wine
4	thin lemon slices

1. Prepare grill.

2. In a small bowl combine crushed peppercorns with Worcestershire and lemon juice. Stir well and set aside.

3. Rub tuna steaks with 1 teaspoon oil and grill to desired degree of doneness (about 5 minutes per side for 1-inch steaks cooked medium).

4. While steaks are grilling, heat remaining oil in a nonstick skillet over medium-high heat. Stir in peppercorn mixture and quickly pour in broth and wine. Cook over high heat, stirring often, for about 3 minutes or until sauce begins to turn light brown. Reduce heat to low.

5. Remove tuna from grill, lay in skillet and sauté only long enough to coat both sides with peppercorn sauce. Divide tuna among warmed plates, spoon remaining sauce over tuna, and serve garnished with lemon slices.

SERVES 4

APPROXIMATELY 4.0 GRAMS FAT PER SERVING

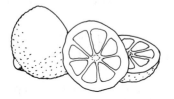

◆ ◆ ◆ ◆ ◆

MARINATED SWORDFISH STEAKS

▶ ▶

I n my opinion, swordfish is one of the best-tasting varieties of fish in the Americas. It comes *this close* to the texture and taste of very delicate meat. One of the best and easily made dishes I know is this platter of swordfish that has been briefly marinated before broiling.

> 4   *swordfish steaks, 1-inch thick (about 1 pound)*
> 2   *tablespoons dry sherry*
> 2   *tablespoons red wine vinegar*
> 2   *teaspoons olive oil*
> 1   *clove garlic, minced*
> ½   *teaspoon hot Hungarian paprika*
> ¼   *cup mixture of chopped fresh cilantro and parsley*
>   *Salt and freshly ground pepper to taste*
>   *Lemon slices or wedges for garnish*

1. Place swordfish in a shallow baking dish in a single layer.

2. Whisk together all remaining ingredients, except salt and pepper, and lemon. Pour marinade over swordfish and refrigerate for 15 minutes, turning fish once.

3. Preheat broiler.

4. Remove baking dish from refrigerator, turn fish again in the marinade and let stand for an additional 15 minutes at room temperature.

5. Broil swordfish 3 to 4 inches from the heat source for about 4 minutes per side, basting once per side with marinade.

---

6. Transfer to a heated serving dish, sprinkle with salt and pepper to taste, and serve garnished with lemon.

SERVES 4
APPROXIMATELY 7.0 GRAMS FAT PER SERVING

◆ ◆ ◆ ◆ ◆

SOLE OLÉ!

▶ ▶

Tequila is a colorless, sweet-tasting liquor made by fermenting and distilling the sweep sap of the agave plant. Legend has it the drink originated in Tequila, Mexico; hence the name. Most tequilas imported to the United States range from 80 proof to an eye-crossing 100-plus proof. But not to worry. In this recipe the alcohol will evaporate in the cooking. The only hangover you'll get is the totally enjoyable one that comes from the delightful flavor and aroma of the agave juice.

In addition to tequila, the recipe calls for ground coriander, fresh cilantro, hot pepper sauce, and fresh lime, which combine to make the Mexican accent even more pronounced.

	Vegetable oil cooking spray
1¼	pounds sole fillets
2	teaspoons fresh lemon juice
	Salt and freshly ground pepper to taste
½	cup Low Fat Chicken Broth (page 43) or canned low-sodium broth
	Juice and grated zest from 1 lime
2	teaspoons cornstarch
½	teaspoon hot pepper sauce, or to taste
1½	teaspoons sugar
½	teaspoon ground coriander
2	tablespoons tequila
2	tablespoons chopped fresh cilantro
	Lime wedges for garnish

---

1. Preheat broiler.

2. Lightly coat a shallow baking dish large enough to hold the fish in a single layer with cooking spray. Add sole and sprinkle with lemon juice, salt if desired, and pepper. Broil for about 3 minutes a side or until fish flakes easily when pierced with a fork.

3. While fish broils, combine broth in a small saucepan with lime juice and zest, cornstarch, hot pepper sauce, sugar, and coriander. Cook over medium heat, stirring, until thickened. Stir in tequila, bring to a boil, and remove saucepan from heat.

4. Transfer fish to a heated serving platter. Pour sauce over fish, sprinkle with cilantro, and garnish with lime wedges.

SERVES 4

APPROXIMATELY 2.2 GRAMS FAT PER SERVING

◆ ◆ ◆ ◆ ◆

BAKED SCROD FILLETS

▶ ▶

In this recipe the fish bakes slowly on a complex flavor base of sautéed vegetables, to which wine, olives, and parsley are added. The flavorings in this dish are calculated to heighten rather than cloak the assertive dignity of the scrod.

1¹/₄	pounds scrod fillet, in one or two pieces
1	tablespoon fresh lemon juice
	Salt and freshly ground pepper to taste
1	teaspoon olive oil
¹/₂	cup chopped onion
¹/₂	cup sliced or chopped celery
2	medium cloves garlic, minced
1	large carrot, diced
1¹/₂	cups chopped plum tomatoes, fresh or no-salt-added canned and drained
¹/₂	cup dry white wine
5	large black olives, rinsed, drained, and pitted
2	tablespoons chopped fresh parsley

1. Preheat oven to 325°F.

2. Sprinkle fish with lemon juice, salt, and pepper and set aside.

3. Heat oil in large nonstick skillet. Add onion, celery, and garlic and cook over medium-low heat, stirring often, for about 5 minutes or until onion is translucent. Add carrot, tomatoes, wine, and olives to skillet and cook over medium

heat, stirring occasionally, for about 20 minutes. Taste and adjust seasonings, if necessary.

4. Stir in parsley and spoon half of the tomato mixture into the bottom of a shallow baking dish. Gently place fish on top and cover with remaining sauce.

5. Bake, uncovered, for about 15 minutes or until fish is tender.

SERVES 4

APPROXIMATELY 3.2 GRAMS FAT PER SERVING

◆ ◆ ◆ ◆ ◆

MUSSELS MARINARA

▶ ▶

When presented piping hot, there is as much pleasure for the eye as for the palate in the plump ivory or amber mussel within its glossy ebony shell set against the fiery exuberance of tomato sauce.

2   *teaspoons olive oil*
4   *cloves garlic, flattened*
2   *large shallots, minced*
    Pinch dried oregano
    Pinch dried thyme
2   *cups dry white wine*
1   *28-ounce can no-salt-added plum tomatoes,*
    drained, chopped, juice reserved
1   *bay leaf*
    Salt and freshly ground pepper to taste
4   *dozen fresh mussels, scrubbed and debearded*

1. Heat oil in a skillet, add garlic and shallots and sauté over low heat, stirring frequently, until shallots are wilted.

2. Add oregano and thyme to skillet and raise heat. Pour in white wine and stir to blend. Bring to a boil, then reduce heat and simmer for 5 minutes.

3. Add tomatoes with about ¼ cup of reserved juice, the bay leaf, and salt and pepper. Cook over medium heat, stirring occasionally, for 10 minutes.

4. Add mussels, cover, and raise heat to medium-high. Cook for about 5 minutes or until mussels open, shaking pan occasionally.

5. Divide among warmed bowls, discarding any mussels that have not opened, and serve.

SERVES **4**

APPROXIMATELY **5.**0 GRAMS FAT PER SERVING

◆ ◆ ◆ ◆ ◆

SHRIMP AND SCALLOPS ON CARROT NESTS

▶ ▶

Nutmeg-scented carrots serve as the canvas for a vibrant composition of shellfish with accents of wine, lemon, garlic, scallions, and fresh herbs, making for a gentle explosion of complementary flavors.

2   teaspoons vegetable oil
1   clove garlic, minced
6   scallions, white and tender greens, coarsely chopped
1/2 pound large shrimp, shelled and deveined
2   large carrots, peeled lengthwise into ribbons (use a vegetable parer)
     Pinch ground nutmeg
1/2 pound small scallops or large scallops halved, rinsed
     Juice of 1 large lemon
1/2 cup dry white wine
1   teaspoon chopped fresh thyme or 1/2 teaspoon dried
1   tablespoon chopped fresh parsley
     Salt and freshly ground pepper to taste

1. Bring a cup of water to a boil in a medium saucepan.

2. Heat oil in a nonstick wok or skillet. Add garlic, scallions, and shrimp to wok and cook over medium heat, stirring lightly, for about 3 minutes.

3. Meanwhile, drop carrots into boiling water and

blanch for about 2 minutes or until just limp. Drain quickly, sprinkle with nutmeg, toss, and cover to keep warm.

4. Add scallops, lemon juice, wine, thyme, parsley, and salt and pepper to wok, cover, and simmer lightly for about 3 minutes. The scallops will cook quickly and the shrimp should be just pink all over.

5. Arrange carrots into "nests" by placing a mound on each plate and making a depression in the center with the back of a large spoon. Using a slotted spoon, transfer an equal amount of shrimp and scallop mixture into the depression of each nest.

6. Raise heat in pan to high and boil remaining sauce for 1 minute. Pour sauce over fish and serve immediately.

SERVES 4

APPROXIMATELY 3.8 GRAMS FAT PER SERVING

◆ ◆ ◆ ◆ ◆

SEAFOOD CREOLE

▶ ▶

𝕮reole dishes traditionally blend chopped celery, onions, and sweet peppers of any color. Garlic, tomatoes, and hot peppers may also be added to these three musketeers of aromatics. The hot peppers can be in the form of a sauce, flakes, or, as suggested here, powdered cayenne. Authentic dishes of the Bayou usually call for lard, salt fatback, or slab bacon, but just a hint of olive oil is used in this low fat Creole.

2	teaspoons olive oil
1	cup chopped onion
3	large cloves garlic, chopped
2	stalks celery, chopped or sliced
$1/2$	cup chopped green bell pepper
$1/2$	cup chopped red or yellow bell pepper
1	teaspoon mild paprika
$1/4$	teaspoon cayenne, or to taste
1	cup dry white wine
1	28-ounce can no-salt-added tomatoes, undrained, coarsely chopped, or 3 cups peeled, chopped fresh tomatoes, juice reserved
1	dozen littleneck clams, scrubbed
2	dozen mussels, scrubbed and debearded
$1/2$	pound medium shrimp, shelled and deveined
2	tablespoons chopped fresh parsley

1. Heat oil in large nonstick pot. Add onion, garlic, celery, and bell peppers and cook over medium-low heat,

stirring often, for about 10 minutes or until onion is translucent and peppers begin to soften.

2. Sprinkle mixture with paprika and cayenne and stir to blend. Raise heat to medium-high, add wine and tomatoes with juice, and cook, stirring occasionally, for 10 minutes.

3. Lower heat slightly and lay in clams and mussels. Cover and simmer gently for 3 minutes. Add shrimp, cover, and cook for an additional 5 minutes or until shrimp is thoroughly pink and mussels and clams have opened.

4. Discarding any mollusks that have not opened, transfer Creole to a heated serving dish, sprinkle with parsley, and serve immediately.

SERVES 4 GENEROUSLY

APPROXIMATELY 4.5 GRAMS FAT PER SERVING

◆ ◆ ◆ ◆ ◆

SHRIMP WITH WINE, GARLIC, AND SHALLOTS

▶ ▶

My friend Beverly, who lives in southern California, is one of the most fat-obsessed people I know. She has a theory that contends, in essence, that there are only so many "fat molecules" in the world. And when one being (human or otherwise) incorporates one of these fat molecules into its system, another being (human or otherwise) sheds a molecule. So, she theorizes, there will always be a balance of fat to distribute.

One way of reducing your share of fat may well be to adapt my light version of shrimp with wine, garlic, and shallots.

>   Olive oil cooking spray
> 1   teaspoon olive oil
> 2   large shallots, minced
> 3   large cloves garlic, halved and flattened
> 1   cup dry white wine
> 1/2   cup Low Fat Chicken Broth (page 43) or canned low-sodium broth
> 1   pound medium-large shrimp, shelled and deveined
>   Salt and freshly ground pepper to taste
>   Juice of 1 large lemon

1. Heat oil in a large skillet coated with cooking spray. Add shallots and garlic and cook over medium-low heat, stirring frequently, until shallots are wilted and garlic begins to turn golden.

2. Raise heat to high, add wine and broth, and cook until liquid starts to boil. Lower heat and simmer for 2 minutes.

3. Add shrimp, stirring to coat well with liquid, cover, and cook for 4 minutes or until shrimp turns pink.

4. Using a slotted spoon, transfer shrimp to a serving dish and sprinkle with salt, pepper, and lemon juice. Spoon liquid from skillet over shrimp and serve.

SERVES 4
APPROXIMATELY 4.0 GRAMS FAT PER SERVING

♦ ♦ ♦ ♦ ♦

HOT AND SWEET SHRIMP

▶ ▶

This dish is a delicious example of Yin-Yang—the Oriental philosophy in which opposites attract and complement each other.

Team it up with plain white rice and a salad of crisp bean sprouts dressed with low-sodium soy sauce and rice vinegar and sprinkled with toasted sesame seeds and minced cilantro. Offer chop sticks and some good Chinese or Japanese beer.

1	pound large shrimp, shelled and deveined
2	teaspoons sugar
3	canned jalapeño peppers, drained, or to taste
2	teaspoons vegetable oil
2	cloves garlic, minced
1/2	teaspoon hot red pepper flakes, or to taste
1	cup pineapple chunks, fresh or canned, unsweetened
1/2	teaspoon salt, or to taste
1	tablespoon cornstarch
3/4	cup water
1	teaspoon low sodium soy sauce
1	teaspoon freshly ground pepper

1. Rinse shrimp and pat dry. Dredge shrimp in sugar and let stand for 5 minutes.

2. Cut jalapeños in half, rinse, and set aside. (For a milder dish, soak peppers in a bowl of water for 5 minutes to remove pungency.)

3. Heat oil in a nonstick wok or skillet and sauté garlic over medium heat until lightly browned. Raise heat, add jalapeños, hot pepper flakes, and pineapple, and cook, stirring, for 1 minute. Add shrimp and salt and stir-fry for 3 minutes, shaking pan several times.

4. Dissolve cornstarch in water and add to shrimp together with soy sauce and pepper. Stir until sauce thickens.

5. Transfer to a heated serving dish and serve immediately.

SERVES 4
APPROXIMATELY 4.5 GRAMS FAT PER SERVING

PASTA and GRAINS

BAKED SPINACH-STUFFED SHELLS

▶ ▶

For a delicious and festive lunch or supper, try these stuffed shells coupled with your favorite green salad. And for a more unusual taste, substitute a bunch of Swiss chard for the spinach.

After cooking, serve at once. If desired top each dish with a teaspoon of grated Parmesan cheese (.5 gram fat per serving).

1	teaspoon olive oil
¹/₂	pound fresh mushrooms, wiped clean, trimmed, and coarsely chopped
1	medium onion or 3 large shallots, coarsely chopped
2	medium cloves garlic, quartered
¹/₄	cup dry white wine
1¹/₄	cups low fat ricotta cheese
1	teaspoon sun-dried or regular tomato paste
1	pound fresh spinach, trimmed, rinsed, steamed, and well drained
¹/₂	teaspoon dried marjoram
¹/₂	teaspoon dried thyme
	Salt and freshly ground pepper to taste
³/₄	pound large pasta shells for stuffing
3	cups Thick and Rich Tomato Sauce (page 3) or canned low sodium tomato sauce
4	teaspoons Parmesan cheese (optional)

1. Heat oil in a large nonstick skillet or saucepan. Add mushrooms, onion or shallots, and garlic and cook over low

heat, stirring often, for 5 minutes. If mixture begins to stick, add a few tablespoons water. Raise heat, add wine, and cook until mushrooms are soft and liquid has evaporated.

2. Cool mixture slightly and transfer to a food processor. Add ricotta cheese, and tomato paste and process until well blended. Add spinach and herbs and process only until spinach is chopped. Taste and season with salt and pepper, if desired. Set stuffing mixture aside.

3. Preheat oven to 350°F.

4. Cook shells according to package directions until slightly underdone. Drain and separate shells so that they don't stick within one another.

5. Using a large spoon, fill shells with stuffing mixture and place, open side up, in a shallow baking dish. Pour tomato sauce over stuffed shells and bake, covered, for 20 minutes or until heated through and bubbly. Top with Parmesan cheese, if desired.

SERVES 4 GENEROUSLY

APPROXIMATELY 6.9 GRAMS FAT PER SERVING WITHOUT
  PARMESAN

◆ ◆ ◆ ◆ ◆

LINGUINE WITH BABY CLAMS

▶ ▶

F̲or this recipe, you'll need the tiniest littlenecks you can find, or perhaps your fishmonger may be able to provide you with itty bitty, delicate Manilla clams.

This is a tomatoless sauce enhanced by lemon and hot pepper. Try it with a salad of radicchio, chicory, and Belgian endive.

1	tablespoon olive oil
3	large cloves garlic, peeled and flattened
1	small dried hot red pepper pod or ¹/₂ teaspoon flakes
20	tiny littleneck or Manilla clams in shell, well scrubbed
¹/₂	cup dry white wine
³/₄	pound linguine
1	cup Low Fat Chicken Broth (page 43) or canned low sodium broth
	Juice of ¹/₂ large lemon
1	teaspoon chopped fresh oregano or ¹/₂ teaspoon dried
¹/₄	teaspoon salt or to taste
	Freshly ground pepper to taste
2	tablespoons chopped fresh parsley

1. In a deep skillet large enough to hold all the clams in one layer or in a large pot, heat oil over medium heat until hot but not smoking. Add garlic and sauté gently until lightly golden but not brown (lower heat if garlic starts to color immediately).

---

2. Break open the hot pepper pod, sprinkle seeds over the garlic, and drop the pod into the oil. Add clams and ¼ cup wine to skillet, turn the heat up to medium-high, and cover to steam the clams open, shaking the pan frequently.

3. As the clams steam, slide the pasta into boiling water and stir until the water returns to a boil. Cook pasta al dente.

4. While the pasta cooks, check the clams and transfer them as they open to a bowl and cover with foil to keep warm.

5. When all clams are steamed, remove and discard the pepper pod, add the broth and remaining wine to the skillet, and cook over medium-high heat for 5 to 7 minutes or until liquid is slightly reduced. Add lemon juice, oregano, salt, and two or three grindings of pepper to the skillet and stir quickly.

6. Drain pasta well and add to skillet, tossing or stirring to coat, and sprinkle with parsley. Divide pasta among warmed bowls, arrange clams on top, and serve.

SERVES 4

APPROXIMATELY 6.2 GRAMS FAT PER SERVING

◆ ◆ ◆ ◆ ◆

WONTON RAVIOLI
WITH HERBED CHEESE FILLING

▶ ▶

This recipe is not culture-shock gone to the kitchen. Rather, it's an easy way of avoiding the time-consuming ordeal of making ravioli from scratch. It eliminates the tedious measuring and cutting (and possible botching up) of homemade pasta dough by substituting store-bought fresh or frozen wonton skins or wrappers. Wonton skins are a fun food item with which to experiment, and with a little practice, a worthwhile shortcut for many inventive creations.

I like to serve this refreshing pasta with spinach, Swiss chard, or broccoli rape just blanched then lightly sautéed with garlic, salt, pepper, and fresh lemon juice.

> 1¹/₄   *cups low fat ricotta*
> 1   *ounce very lean ham (95% fat free), thinly sliced and slivered*
> 1   *tablespoon finely chopped fresh basil or 1¹/₂ teaspoons dried*
> 1   *teaspoon finely chopped fresh thyme or ¹/₂ teaspoon dried*
> 1   *egg, lightly beaten*
>   *Salt and freshly ground pepper to taste*
> 40   *wonton wrappers (available in most large grocery stores or Chinese markets), defrosted if frozen*
>   *Flour*

3   cups Thick and Rich Tomato Sauce (page 3) or
    canned low sodium tomato sauce
    Chopped fresh parsley or basil for garnish

1. To make the filling, combine ricotta, ham, basil, thyme, and egg in a small bowl. Stir with a fork to blend. Taste and add salt and pepper, if desired.

2. To assemble, lay wonton wrappers on a work surface and cover with a damp kitchen towel. Lightly flour work area and lay one wrapper on floured surface. Keep remaining wrappers covered, as they dry out quickly.

3. Place about a tablespoon of filling in the center of wrapper, moisten the edges with water and lay a second wrapper on top, pushing from filling outward to remove as much air as possible. Seal edges with light pressure and trim with knife or cookie cutter into an attractive shape, if desired. As the ravioli is finished, lay on a piece of paper toweling or a kitchen towel to dry *slightly*. Continue until you have made 20 ravioli.

4. Reheat sauce if necessary.

5. Bring water to a very slow boil in a large pot and add the ravioli a few at a time. The water must not boil too rapidly or the ravioli may fall apart. Cook gently for about 4 minutes or until the ravioli rise to the surface. Remove with a slotted spoon to a warm platter as they are cooked.

6. Divide ravioli among heated plates, spoon sauce over, sprinkle with basil or parsley, and serve.

SERVES 4
APPROXIMATELY 5.5 GRAMS FAT PER SERVING

◆ ◆ ◆ ◆ ◆

FETTUCCINE
WITH SHRIMP AND SCALLOPS

▶ ▶

I never tire of thinking, talking, or writing about food. What I do find exhausting is avoiding or eliminating some long-cherished favorites. However, if it is true that necessity is the mother of invention, then, in my opinion, creativity is the salvation of low fat recipes.

Recently I recreated one of those old favorites, wanting to retain the rich creamy texture and flavor of the original but without the artery-spackling combo of butter, egg yolks, and cream. My new Fettuccine with Shrimp and Scallops is the result.

   3/4 pound fettuccine
   1   teaspoon olive oil
   2   cloves garlic, chopped
   1   shallot, minced
   *1   cup Low Fat Chicken Broth (page 43) or canned
         low sodium broth*
   1/2 pound medium shrimp, shelled and deveined
   1/2 pound sea scallops, cut in half if very large
   1 1/2 tablespoons no-salt-added tomato paste
   1 1/2 tablespoons all-purpose flour
   1/2 cup nonfat dry milk
         Salt and freshly ground pepper to taste
   1   tablespoon chopped fresh chives (optional)

1. Slide fettuccine into boiling water.
2. While pasta cooks, heat oil in a large nonstick skillet

or pot over medium-low heat and sauté garlic and shallot, stirring often, until shallot is translucent. Do not allow garlic to brown. If mixture sticks, add a tablespoon of broth.

3. Add ¼ cup broth to pan, add shrimp and scallops and sauté for 2 to 4 minutes or until shrimp are turning pink. Using a slotted spoon, remove shrimp and scallops from skillet and set aside.

4. Stir tomato paste into pan and cook for 1 minute or until blended. Sprinkle with flour and stir for 30 seconds to dissolve.

5. Sprinkle in nonfat dry milk, stirring to combine. Add remaining broth and simmer over medium heat for about 7 minutes or until slightly thickened. Taste and add salt and pepper, if desired.

6. Return shrimp and scallops to pan and cook over low heat for about 3 minutes or until fish is cooked through; do not boil. Divide cooked pasta and shrimp mixture among warmed bowls, sprinkle with chopped chives, if desired, and serve.

SERVES 4

APPROXIMATELY 4.9 GRAMS FAT PER SERVING

◆ ◆ ◆ ◆ ◆

PASTA
WITH CREAMED VEGETABLES

▶ ▶

Everyone loves this dish! The pasta can be penne, linguine, shells, or your favorite variety. The vegetables can be changed according to taste, availability, and whim.

$1/4$	cup thinly sliced carrots
$1/4$	cup julienne-sliced red bell pepper
$1/2$	cup snow peas
$3/4$	pound pasta
2	teaspoons olive oil
2	large cloves garlic, minced
1	shallot, minced
$1/4$	cup sliced fresh mushrooms, wiped clean
1	tablespoon no-salt-added tomato paste
1	tablespoon all-purpose flour
$3/4$	cup low fat (1%) milk
4	ounces low fat ricotta cheese
1	tablespoon freshly grated Romano cheese
$1/4$	cup artichoke hearts, canned in water or frozen and thawed

1. Heat about $3/4$ cup water in a medium saucepan. When water boils, add carrots, cover, and steam for about 3 minutes, then add red pepper and cook for an additional 2 minutes. Add snow peas and cook for another 2 minutes. Drain and set vegetables aside.

2. Slide pasta into boiling water.

3. In a large saucepan, sauté garlic, shallot, carrots, red pepper, and snow peas in oil over low heat until garlic and shallot are soft. Add mushrooms and sauté until they begin to give up their liquid. Stir in tomato paste and cook for 1 minute to blend.

4. Add flour to saucepan with vegetable mixture, stirring briefly to dissolve. Add milk and cook, stirring, until thickened. Do not boil.

5. Remove saucepan from heat and stir in cheeses, beating well with a wooden spoon. Return pan to stove and heat mixture through over very low heat. Drain pasta, toss with sauce, and serve.

SERVES 4
APPROXIMATELY 5.9 GRAMS FAT PER SERVING

◆ ◆ ◆ ◆ ◆

PASTA PUTTANESCA

▶ ▶

Did you hear about the chef who gave his dog some garlic and now his bark is worse than his bite? Pasta Puttanesca, or "harlot's pasta," boasts a brazen amount of garlic, no doubt reflecting the lusty, uninhibited nature of its namesake. With no trace of bark or bite, Pasta Puttanesca exudes an abundance of flavor, fragrance, and great good looks, and is one of the best hastily made dishes in creation.

Although I've drastically reduced the amount of olive oil normally used in preparing the classic sauce, you are free to vary the amount of garlic and hot pepper according to your own threshold for it. But beware of adding more olives, capers, or anchovies. They will greatly alter the flavor, and the fat and sodium content can grow to humongous proportions.

This dish is traditionally served without grated cheese, but pass lots of crusty bread to mop up the sauce.

> 1 *teaspoon olive oil*
> 5 *anchovy fillets, rinsed, drained, and torn into small pieces*
> 4 *large cloves garlic, coarsely chopped, or to taste*
> 10 *black olives, preferably Gaeta, pitted and halved*
> 1 *tablespoon capers, rinsed and drained*
> 1 *small dried hot red pepper or ¹/₂ teaspoon hot red pepper flakes, or to taste*
> 1 *28-ounce can no-salt-added plum tomatoes, undrained*

³/₄   *pound linguine or thick spaghetti*
     Pinch dried oregano
     Freshly ground pepper to taste
2   *tablespoons chopped fresh Italian parsley*

1. Heat oil in a large, deep nonstick skillet and add anchovies, stirring over medium heat to dissolve. Add garlic, olives, and capers, and cook, stirring and pressing olives flat, for about 2 minutes or until garlic begins to turn golden. Break open hot pepper and sprinkle flakes into skillet. Discard pod.

2. Raise heat to high and add tomatoes, large spoonfuls at a time, to skillet. Stand back—it will splatter. Crush the tomatoes with the side of the spoon as you put them into the skillet. Continue until all tomatoes are crushed and cooking. Reserve any leftover juice in the can.

3. Slide pasta into boiling water.

4. Sprinkle tomato sauce with oregano and a few grindings of black pepper and simmer over medium-high heat, stirring occasionally, until pasta is cooked. If sauce seems dry, add a small amount of the reserved tomato juice.

5. Drain pasta well, add to the sauce if the skillet is large enough, or toss well in a large, warm bowl. Sprinkle with parsley and serve immediately.

SERVES 4

APPROXIMATELY 4.5 GRAMS FAT PER SERVING

◆ ◆ ◆ ◆ ◆

PENNE WITH MUSHROOMS AND ASPARAGUS

▶ ▶

Penne—a large, straight tube of macaroni cut on the diagonal to resemble a quill—is a sturdy pasta that stands up to heavy sauces, as opposed to the light sauces often combined with delicate pastas such as cappellini.

As to the dish at hand, after trying in vain for years to pry this recipe from the restaurant in Chicago where I'd eaten it, I came up with my own rendition—equally good, in my opinion, but kinder to the arteries, I'm sure.

$3/4$ *pound fresh slim asparagus, tough stems trimmed*
$3/4$ *pound penne or other tubular pasta*
1   *teaspoon margarine*
1   *large shallot, finely chopped*
10   *ounces fresh mushrooms, wiped clean, trimmed, and sliced*
2   *tablespoons flour*
$1^1/2$ *cups low fat (1%) milk*
3   *tablespoons nonfat dry milk*
$1/4$ *cup freshly grated Romano cheese*
     Freshly ground pepper to taste

1. Steam asparagus, covered, for about 3 minutes or until nearly tender but still bright green. Rinse under cold water, cut into $1^1/2$-inch lengths, and set aside.

2. Slide pasta into boiling water.

3. While pasta cooks, heat margarine in a large, nonstick skillet and sauté shallot over medium-low heat, stirring

often, until well wilted. Add mushrooms and cook until mushrooms are wilted and have given up their liquid. Sprinkle with flour and stir for about 30 seconds or until flour is dissolved.

4. Add milk and nonfat dry milk and whisk or stir to blend. Do not allow mixture to boil. Cook gently until slightly thickened. Stir in asparagus and heat through.

5. Drain pasta and add to skillet if there's room, or transfer mixture to a large, hot bowl. Add Romano and toss to blend. Serve immediately, passing pepper grinder separately.

SERVES 4

APPROXIMATELY 4.9 GRAMS FAT PER SERVING

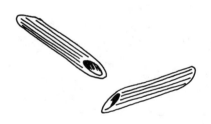

♦ ♦ ♦ ♦ ♦

PASTA SALAD PRIMAVERA

▶ ▶

I serve this dish to my vegetarian friends—and to all the rest who are into plain old good eating. Healthy, colorful, and texturally interesting, this is a love-match between pasta and crisp-steamed vegetables.

Excellent as a one-dish meal or as part of a buffet, I also like to take it along on picnics or to the office.

3/4	pound fusilli or corkscrew pasta
6	tablespoons Low Fat Chicken Broth (page 43) or canned low-sodium broth
1	small zucchini, cut into 1/2-inch slices
1	small yellow squash, cut into 1/2-inch slices
2	cups sugar snap peas
6	tablespoons cider vinegar
2	teaspoons water
2	teaspoons fresh lemon juice
1	tablespoon chopped fresh dillweed or 1/2 tablespoon dried
1	teaspoon Dijon mustard
3	teaspoons oil
	Salt and freshly ground pepper to taste
1	medium red bell pepper, cut into julienne strips
1	medium red onion, diced
3	ripe plum tomatoes at room temperature, quartered
2	ounces low fat mozzarella, cut into thick "toothpicks"
2	large fresh basil leaves, slivered or torn in pieces

1. Cook pasta according to package directions, drain, toss with 1 tablespoon broth, and set aside to cool to room temperature.

2. In a large pot, steam zucchini and yellow squash for 5 minutes, then add snap peas and steam for an additional 3 minutes. Cool vegetables to room temperature.

3. Combine vinegar, water, lemon juice, remaining broth, dill, and mustard. Whisk in oil 1 teaspoon at a time. Taste and add salt and pepper, if desired.

4. Pour dressing over pasta, add steamed vegetables, bell pepper, onion, tomatoes, and cheese. Toss until well blended, sprinkle with basil, and serve.

SERVES 4

APPROXIMATELY 7.6 GRAMS FAT PER SERVING

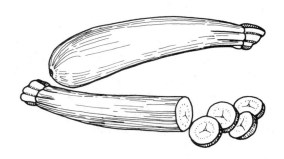

◆ ◆ ◆ ◆

CONFETTI RICE SALAD

▶ ▶

I have always thought of cooking as an exciting adventure, one that would lead me down paths of gastronomic delight. Of course, that has not always been the case. I've hit more dead ends than I care to remember. But the successes have compensated for many mistakes. Some years ago, one such expedition yielded happy results. It is the Confetti Rice Salad I've outlined below. The concept is basic: create a salad composed of a simple blend of rice and vegetables and bring it all together with a good, assertive dressing.

This dish makes a rather flamboyant presentation when served on its own, or as an accompaniment to fish or fowl. It is also wonderful as part of a buffet layout.

1	cup uncooked long-grain white rice
1¼	cups water
1	cup Low Fat Chicken Broth (page 43) or canned low-sodium broth
	Salt and freshly ground pepper to taste
2	teaspoons minced fresh parsley
½	cup green peas, fresh or frozen and thawed
½	cup golden corn kernels, fresh or frozen and thawed
¼	cup finely sliced scallions, white and tender greens
¼	cup drained, diced pimientos
2	tablespoons red wine vinegar
2	teaspoons olive oil
1	small clove garlic, pressed

1. In a saucepan, combine rice, water, $3/4$ cup chicken broth, salt and pepper, and parsley. Bring to a boil, then reduce heat, cover, and simmer gently for 35 minutes.

2. Stir in peas and corn, cover, and continue cooking over low heat for an additional 5 to 10 minutes or until rice is tender and liquid is evaporated. Transfer to a mixing bowl and cool to room temperature.

3. Add scallions and pimientos to rice and toss lightly to blend. Refrigerate for at least 2 hours or until well chilled.

4. Combine remaining $1/4$ cup chicken broth with vinegar, oil, and garlic in a jar with a tight-fitting lid. Shake until mixture is thoroughly blended. Pour over chilled rice and toss lightly to coat grains. Taste and correct seasonings, if necessary.

SERVES 4 AS A SIDE DISH
APPROXIMATELY 3.8 GRAMS FAT PER SERVING

◆ ◆ ◆ ◆ ◆

BROWN AND WILD RICE
WITH PEAS AND MUSHROOMS

▶ ▶

Although my Brown and Wild Rice with Peas and Mushrooms is not a twist on that divine Venetian dish called *risi e bisi*, it too begs for the flavor and delicacy of good homemade broth. This side dish does well with nearly every entrée of meat, fish, or fowl, along with a green steamed vegetable or a salad.

1	teaspoon olive oil
2	cloves garlic, coarsely minced
1	small onion, chopped
1	cup clean, thinly sliced mushrooms
1½	cups Low Fat Chicken Broth (*page 43*), or canned low sodium broth
1½	cups water
¾	cup uncooked brown rice
½	cup uncooked wild rice
	Salt and freshly ground pepper to taste
¾	cup green peas, fresh or frozen and thawed

1. Heat oil in a large saucepan. Add garlic and cook over medium heat until lightly browned. Remove pan from heat and stir in onion and mushrooms.

2. Add chicken broth and water and stir in brown and wild rice. Season with salt and pepper.

3. Return saucepan to heat, bring mixture to a boil, then cover, reduce heat, and simmer for 35 minutes, adding a

small amount of water during cooking, if necessary, to keep rice from sticking.

4. Stir in green peas, and continue to cook, covered, for an additional 10 minutes or until rice is tender.

SERVES 4 AS A SIDE DISH

APPROXIMATELY 2.5 GRAMS FAT PER SERVING

◆ ◆ ◆ ◆ ◆

VEGETABLE PAELLA

▶ ▶

One of the many bonuses of this recipe is not immediately evident. And that is its preparation time, which is
definitely not proportionate to the number of ingredients it
contains. It is a dish that can be completed in well under 45
minutes from start to finish.

Paella is a complete meal; however, it does extremely
well with a salad—try one composed of orange slices, red
onion rings, and a sprinkling of black olives.

2   *teaspoons olive oil*

1   *large onion, chopped*

4   *large cloves garlic, minced*

2   *cups no-salt-added canned, drained and chopped
tomatoes, juice reserved*

3   *leeks, white and 1 inch of tender greens, well
rinsed and chopped*

1   *14-ounce can water-packed artichokes, drained*

1   *large red bell pepper, seeded and cut into julienne
strips*

1   *large green bell pepper, seeded and cut into
julienne strips*

6   *stalks fresh asparagus, trimmed and cut in pieces*

$^1/_2$ *cup golden corn, fresh or frozen and thawed*

1   *cup sliced sugar snap peas, fresh or frozen and
thawed*

4   *cups plus 2 tablespoons Low Fat Chicken Broth
(page 43) or canned low-sodium broth*

1   *cup dry white wine*

1¹/₂ cups uncooked white rice
¹/₂ teaspoon crushed saffron threads
2 tablespoons chopped fresh basil or parsley

1. Heat oil in large nonstick pot over medium-low heat and sauté onion and garlic, stirring often, for about 5 minutes or until onion is well wilted but not browned.

2. Stir in tomatoes, leeks, artichokes, red and green peppers, asparagus, corn, snap peas, and 1 cup broth. Raise heat and simmer for 5 minutes.

3. Add wine, 3 cups broth, ¹/₂ cup reserved tomato juice, and rice. Bring to a boil, cover, reduce heat and simmer for 25 minutes or until rice is cooked through.

4. While rice cooks, soak saffron threads in 2 tablespoons of heated broth. When rice is done, add saffron and broth mixture and stir well to blend. Garnish with fresh basil or parsley and divide among heated bowls.

SERVES 4

APPROXIMATELY 6.6 GRAMS FAT PER SERVING

◆ ◆ ◆ ◆ ◆

RISOTTO MILANESE

▶ ▶

Risotto is a uniquely Italian dish in which hot stock or broth is stirred into a mixture of Arborio rice that has been sautéed in butter. Stock is added, little by little, and the mixture is stirred continually while it cooks until all the liquid is absorbed.

This process of adding stock until absorbed is definitely labor-intensive. But the results are justified: rice that is delectably creamy with grains remaining separate and firm. Sometimes enhanced with chicken, shellfish, mushrooms, vegetables, or cheese, the risotto below is scented with that wonderful aromatic spice, saffron.

Risotto Milanese is classically served with braised veal shanks, but it is an absolute knockout as a first course or with a simply roasted chicken or turkey, or braised meat or fowl, and a salad of fresh arugula with Mustard Vinaigrette with Sherry (page 11).

3	cups low sodium vegetable broth
	Vegetable oil cooking spray
1	teaspoon olive oil
1	large shallot, chopped
1¹/₂	cups uncooked Italian Arborio rice
¹/₄	teaspoon crushed saffron threads soaked in ¹/₄ cup of hot broth
¹/₄	cup chopped fresh parsley
¹/₄	cup freshly grated Parmesan cheese
2	teaspoons butter or margarine, or blend
	Salt and freshly ground pepper to taste

1. In a saucepan, heat broth and place it so it will be readily available. Keep broth simmering.

2. Heat the cooking spray and oil in a deep skillet and sauté the shallot over medium heat, stirring occasionally, until wilted. Pour in the rice and stir to coat with the oil and shallot mixture. Sauté for 2 minutes.

3. Add a ladleful (about ½ cup) of the simmering broth to the rice in the skillet and stir the mixture over medium heat until the broth has been absorbed. Add the saffron and broth in which it has soaked. Continue to stir and add broth by the ladleful, raising the heat slightly if necessary to keep the mixture simmering but not boiling or sticking to the pan, for about 30 minutes or until the rice is creamy outside but still a touch firm to the bite inside. You may not quite use all the broth.

4. When the risotto is very nearly done, stir in the parsley, Parmesan, and butter or margarine, taste and add salt, if desired, and a few grindings of black pepper and serve immediately.

SERVES 4 AS A SIDE DISH
APPROXIMATELY 5.2 GRAMS FAT PER SERVING

◆ ◆ ◆ ◆ ◆

BASMATI RICE AND APPLE SALAD

▶ ▶

$\mathbb{B}$asmati rice is grown in the foothills of the Himalayas. It has a narrow, long grain and a fragrant, nutlike flavor and aroma. *Basmati* means "queen of fragrance," and when it's combined with apples, raisins, herbs, and other flavors, as in the recipe below, it becomes even more aromatic.

1	*large apple, preferably Granny Smith, peeled, cored, and diced*
1	*tablespoon lemon juice*
2	*teaspoons vegetable oil*
2	*tablespoons Low Fat Chicken Broth (page 43) or canned low sodium broth*
2	*tablespoons cider vinegar*
1/4	*cup chopped fresh parsley*
1	*teaspoon chopped fresh tarragon or 1/2 teaspoon dried*
3	*stalks celery, sliced*
21/2	*cups cold, cooked basmati rice*
1/2	*cup golden raisins*
	Salt and freshly ground pepper to taste

1. Toss apple pieces in lemon juice and set aside.

2. Whisk together oil, broth, vinegar, parsley, and tarragon.

---

3. Add celery, rice, raisins, and apples with lemon juice to vinaigrette, tossing to blend. Taste and add salt and pepper, if desired.

SERVES 4 AS A SIDE DISH
APPROXIMATELY 3.2 GRAMS FAT PER SERVING

HERB AND SHALLOT CORN BREAD

▶ ▶

I n this savory version, I've included honey with shallots and various herbs for mouth-watering results. Offered alongside baked chicken, grilled or roasted fish, fowl or meat and salad, this corn bread will round out any dinner. I also enjoy it for breakfast or lunch on its own, washed down with a mug of hot coffee or tea.

1	teaspoon diet margarine
1/2	cup sifted all-purpose flour
1²/₃	cups sifted cornmeal
1	teaspoon baking soda
1	teaspoon baking powder
2	tablespoons nonfat dry milk
1/2	teaspoon each: dried thyme, rosemary, and tarragon (or herbs of your choice)
1	large egg
2	large egg whites
1¹/2	tablespoons honey
1¹/4	cups low fat buttermilk
1¹/4	cups low fat (1%) milk
2	large shallots, finely minced

1. Preheat oven to 350°F. Grease a 9-inch-square baking pan with the margarine.

2. In a small bowl, combine flour, cornmeal, baking soda, baking powder, nonfat dry milk, and herbs.

3. In a large bowl, combine the egg and egg whites,

beating until foamy, then add honey, buttermilk, low-fat milk, and shallots. Add dry ingredients to bowl and blend well.

4. Pour batter into prepared pan and bake for 40 minutes or until a tester inserted in the center of the bread comes out clean.

MAKES NINE 3-INCH SQUARES
APPROXIMATELY 2.5 GRAMS FAT PER SQUARE

◆ ◆ ◆ ◆ ◆

BULGUR AND CORN SALAD
WITH MINT DRESSING

▶ ▶

Serve this refreshing salad with lean grilled steak or chicken or for lunch garnished with lettuce leaves and plump ripe tomatoes.

1	cup bulgur
2¹/₂	cups water
1¹/₂	cups corn kernels, fresh or frozen and thawed
2	sun-dried tomato halves (not oil-packed), chopped
¹/₄	cup chopped fresh cilantro or parsley
¹/₄	cup chopped chives
2	tablespoons coarsely chopped dry-roasted peanuts
3	tablespoons red wine vinegar
3	tablespoons Low Fat Chicken Broth (page 43) or canned low sodium broth
1	tablespoon fresh lemon juice
2	tablespoons chopped fresh mint or 1 tablespoon dried, crushed
1	teaspoon cumin
2	cloves garlic, pressed or finely minced
	Salt and freshly ground pepper to taste

1. Combine bulgur and water in a medium saucepan, bring to a boil, then stir in corn and tomato pieces. Cover saucepan and remove from heat. Let stand, covered, for 30 minutes or until liquid is absorbed and bulgur is tender. Stir in cilantro, chives, and peanuts.

2. In a small bowl, combine vinegar, broth, lemon juice, mint, cumin, and garlic. Stir or whisk well.

3. Add vinaigrette to bulgur mixture and toss gently with a fork to blend. Taste and add salt and pepper, if desired. Serve warm, at room temperature, or chilled.

SERVES 4

APPROXIMATELY 3.9 GRAMS FAT PER SERVING

VEGETABLES

◆ ◆ ◆ ◆ ◆

BRAISED ARTICHOKES ROMAN STYLE

▶ ▶

In this country, the globe or French artichoke is culti-
vated primarily in California's midcoastal region. It is ac-
tually the bud of a large plant belonging to the thistle
family.

Artichokes are available year round, but are at their
peak from March through May. Look for deep green artichokes with tightly closed leaves. Beloved by the French as
artichauts, they are particular favorites of Italians, who take
enormous pleasure in this extraordinary vegetable and
have created many fascinating ways to cook it. One of the
most attractive and appealing is Roman style, which is
highly prized by natives and tourists alike as *carciofi alla
Romana*.

Serve either warm or at room temperature, as a side
dish or first course. Try to prepare the artichokes the same
day you plan to eat them as they lose flavor when refrigerated.

4   *fresh, firm young artichokes or 6 baby artichokes*
3   *large lemons*
2   *teaspoons olive oil*
3   *cloves garlic, minced*
1   *cup coarsely chopped Italian parsley*
$1/2$ *cup coarsely chopped fresh mint*
$1/2$ *cup Low Fat Chicken Broth (page 43) or canned
       low sodium broth
       Salt and freshly ground pepper to taste*

1. Cut off the top ½ inch of each artichoke and remove *all* tough outer leaves (if you are using baby artichokes, there won't be very much to remove). Trim stems to about one inch and pare. As you trim each artichoke, lay it in a bowl of water into which you have squeezed the juice of 1 lemon. It is important to work quickly to keep the artichokes from discoloring. When all artichokes are trimmed and dipped in lemon water, quarter each lengthwise and remove and discard the fuzzy choke, quickly returning the pieces to the lemon water as you work.

2. Drain the artichokes and toss in a bowl with oil, garlic, parsley, mint, and 2 tablespoons of the broth. Place contents of bowl in a deep skillet large enough to hold the artichokes in a single layer. Add remaining broth and enough water to cover the bottom of the skillet to a depth of about ½ inch.

3. Cover and cook the artichokes over medium heat for 20 minutes or until the stems can be easily pierced with a fork.

4. Uncover and raise the heat to reduce most of the remaining liquid. Be careful not to brown the artichokes or they won't be as tender.

5. Transfer artichokes to a serving platter, including any herbs and garlic from the skillet. Squeeze the juice from the 2 remaining lemons over all and sprinkle lightly with salt and pepper to taste.

SERVES 4
APPROXIMATELY 2.8 GRAMS FAT PER SERVING

◆ ◆ ◆ ◆

BAKED FENNEL

▶ ▶

Although there are two types of this aromatic plant, Florence fennel, also known as *finocchio,* is by far the most widely used. Grown throughout the Mediterranean and in the United States, this broad, bulbous-based plant has been stuck with the false moniker "sweet anise," which turns off those of us who harbor an aversion to the taste of licorice. And so much the pity, because its flavor is sweeter and more delicate than anise's.

You have probably seen finocchio, which is available from late fall through early spring in Italian markets or on greengrocers' shelves, or you may have had it raw in salads in Italian restaurants. But if you've never cooked with it, you're missing a good thing; cooked, its unique flavor is even lighter and more subtle than raw.

Baked Fennel is a natural with roasted meats or chicken, and terrific with broiled meat. In fact, there is practically no dish it cannot accompany.

> 2 fennel bulbs (*about 1 pound each with tops*)
> 1 teaspoon olive oil
> 2 large cloves garlic, minced
> ¼ cup dry white wine
> ¼ cup chopped plum tomatoes, fresh or canned no-salt-added, drained
>   Pinch dried thyme
> 3 tablespoons freshly grated Parmesan cheese (*optional at 1.1 grams fat per serving*)
>   Salt and freshly ground pepper to taste

1. Remove tops from fennel and cut bulbs in half lengthwise. Remove and discard center cores.

2. Place bulb halves in a vegetable steamer, cut sides up, cover, and steam for 20 minutes or until nearly tender.

3. Preheat oven to 400°F.

4. While fennel steams, heat oil in a nonstick skillet over medium-low heat and sauté garlic until barely golden. Add wine, raise heat, and bring to a boil. Lower heat to medium, add tomatoes, and simmer for 5 minutes.

5. Transfer contents of skillet to a shallow baking pan. Lay the fennel halves, cut side up, in pan in one layer and spoon a little tomato mixture over them. Sprinkle with thyme, cheese if desired, and salt and pepper to taste. Bake for about 20 minutes or until tops are golden.

SERVES 4

APPROXIMATELY 1.2 GRAMS FAT PER SERVING WITHOUT CHEESE

◆ ◆ ◆ ◆ ◆

CREAMY WHIPPED POTATOES

▶ ▶

Serve this satisfying, low fat version of the traditional comfort food with any and all of your favorite roasted, grilled, or baked meats, fish, or poultry, or as a welcome partner for other vegetables, such as baby peas, spinach, or carrots.

4   potatoes (about 1¼ pounds), peeled and
     quartered
½   cup evaporated low fat milk
¼   cup low fat plain yogurt
½   teaspoon salt, or to taste
     Salt and freshly ground pepper to taste
1   tablespoon minced fresh chives (optional)

1. Boil potatoes (in lightly salted water, if desired) for about 20 minutes or until tender, drain, and return to pot.
2. Heat briefly, shaking pot, to evaporate all moisture. Add milk, yogurt, salt, pepper, and chives if desired, and whip potatoes until creamy.

SERVES 4
APPROXIMATELY 1.3 GRAMS FAT PER SERVING

◆ ◆ ◆ ◆ ◆

BAKED POTATO "PUFFS"

▶ ▶

Bistro-style food has come to mean basic unpretentious dishes served up in a simple, carefree, comfortable setting. For me, these delicious baked potato slices are the epitome of bistro-style food at its tastiest.

The low-low-fat recipe I offer here may be reduced even further by eliminating the grated Parmesan cheese (about .5 gram fat per serving). But the amount of fat meted out is negligible while the flavor it provides is abundant.

Ideal as a side dish, these "puffs" do equally well when matched with most sautéed dishes, or try them as savory hot hors d'oeuvres with cocktails or as snacks to pass around during half time at a Superbowl party.

2   large baking potatoes, scrubbed
2   cloves garlic, finely minced
¹/₄   teaspoon dried oregano
¹/₄   teaspoon dried thyme
¹/₄   teaspoon dried crumbled rosemary
     Salt and freshly ground pepper to taste
     Vegetable oil cooking spray
1   tablespoon freshly grated Parmesan

1. Preheat oven to 400°F.

2. Cut each potato into 5 slices lengthwise and rub the slices together until they become slick with starch (this helps the potatoes puff up during baking).

4. Coat a baking pan lightly with cooking spray. Arrange slices on pan in one layer and bake for 20 minutes.

5. Sprinkle with grated Parmesan and return to oven for an additional 5 to 10 minutes or until fully puffed and golden.

SERVES 4

APPROXIMATELY 1.0 GRAM FAT PER SERVING

◆ ◆ ◆ ◆

CORN-STUFFED RED PEPPERS

▶ ▶

Here is a great way to learn the ABC and E's of nutrition: the corn (even the creamed variety) is high in vitamin A and B and the red pepper is a flavor-packed source of vitamins A, B, C, and E.

This is a lovely accompaniment to roasted meats and fowl.

2	*large red bell peppers*
2	*cups canned cream-style corn*
¹/₂	*cup plus 4 teaspoons fine, dry bread crumbs*
¹/₂	*medium green bell pepper, cored, seeded, and diced*
¹/₄	*cup drained, diced pimientos*
1¹/₂	*tablespoons finely minced scallions or shallots*
2	*teaspoons minced fresh cilantro or parsley*
1	*teaspoon dry mustard*
	Salt and freshly ground pepper to taste

1. Preheat oven to 350°F.

2. Cut red peppers in half lengthwise and remove seeds and white membranes. Drop into a pot with rapidly boiling water for 2 minutes. Remove and plunge into cold water. Drain and set pepper halves aside.

3. Combine corn with all remaining ingredients, except reserved pepper halves and 4 teaspoons bread crumbs. Stir until well blended.

4. Place red pepper halves, cut side up, in a shallow baking pan small enough so that peppers touch one another. Spoon an equal amount of corn mixture into the 4 pepper

halves and sprinkle the top of each with 1 teaspoon bread crumbs. Add water to baking pan to a depth of ¼ inch and bake for 20 minutes, adding a little more water if it evaporates. Serve immediately.

SERVES 4

APPROXIMATELY 1.9 GRAMS FAT PER SERVING

◆ ◆ ◆ ◆ ◆

RIBBONS AND RUBIES

▶ ▶

The ribbons are thin lengths of zucchini, yellow squash, and carrots and the rubies are sun-dried tomatoes.

A wonderful alternative to salad, this dish is also lovely when wed to soup or a sandwich for a light lunch or supper.

6   sun-dried tomato halves (*not* oil-packed)
1   small zucchini
1   small yellow squash
2   medium carrots
2   teaspoons olive oil
2   tablespoons fresh lemon juice
2   fresh basil leaves, slivered
1   teaspoon chopped fresh chives
    Salt and freshly ground pepper to taste

1. Add tomato halves to a saucepan of rapidly boiling water. Cook for about 3 minutes or until softened. Drain, cut into tiny pieces, and transfer to a mixing bowl.

2. Trim ends from zucchini, squash, and carrots and with vegetable parer, peel lengthwise into thin ribbons. Plunge into a small amount of boiling water for about 4 minutes or until wilted but not mushy. Drain.

3. Add squash, carrots, and remaining ingredients to tomatoes in mixing bowl and toss until well blended. Serve immediately.

SERVES 4

APPROXIMATELY 2.9 GRAMS FAT PER SERVING

◆ ◆ ◆ ◆ ◆

BROILED TOMATOES NAPOLI

▶ ▶

This is a very simple recipe for tomatoes: sliced, topped with a bit of lemon juice and capers and napped with a light coat of garlic, basil, bread crumbs, and Romano cheese. Serve the tomatoes hot as a tasty accompaniment to roasts, sautéed or poached meat, fish, or poultry.

4	large, ripe but firm beefsteak tomatoes
	Vegetable oil cooking spray
1	tablespoon fresh lemon juice
1/2	tablespoon capers, rinsed, drained, and chopped
1	clove garlic, finely minced
8	basil leaves, chopped
1/4	cup bread crumbs, preferably made from day-old French bread
2	tablespoons freshly grated Romano cheese

1. Preheat broiler.

2. Cut tomatoes in half and place halves, cut side up, in one layer in a shallow baking dish sprayed with vegetable oil. Drizzle the top of each half with lemon juice and sprinkle with capers.

3. Mix together garlic, basil, bread crumbs, and grated cheese, coat tops of tomatoes with mixture, and broil until crumbs are golden and tomatoes are slightly bubbly. Serve at once or tomatoes will become soggy.

SERVES 4
APPROXIMATELY 1.9 GRAMS FAT PER SERVING

◆ ◆ ◆ ◆ ◆

ROAST VEGETABLE MEDLEY

▶ ▶

Roasting summer vegetables in the home oven—or, if you prefer, grilling them on the outdoor barbecue—is one of the best methods of concentrating their flavor. Suddenly, peppers fulfill their sweet promise; zucchini seems fresher and juicier; red onions caramelize to a savory turn, and slender green beans retain much of their crunchy texture. All come to rest on a luxurious bed of burgundy radicchio leaves, and the scallion vinaigrette brings it all together.

I find this a marvelous party dish, equally suited to a buffet or dining table.

4   scallions, white and tender greens
2   teaspoons canola or other light vegetable oil
1   small red bell pepper, cored, seeded, cut into
    ¹/₂-inch strips
1   small yellow bell pepper, cored, seeded, cut into
    ¹/₂-inch strips
1   large red onion, cut into ³/₄-inch slices
¹/₂ pound green beans, ends trimmed
2   slender zucchini, cut into strips 3 inches long by
    ³/₄ inch wide
1   teaspoon ground cumin
1   teaspoon dried oregano
1   tablespoon fresh lime juice
2   tablespoons red wine vinegar
1   teaspoon coarse mustard

---

¹/₄   cup Low Fat Chicken Broth (page 43), or canned
      low sodium broth
      Salt and freshly ground pepper to taste
1   medium head radicchio

1. Preheat oven to 450°F.
2. Toss scallions with ¹/₂ teaspoon of the oil and arrange on a baking sheet. Roast for about 10 minutes or until brown and softened, turning once or twice. Remove from oven and set aside to cool. Do not turn off oven.
3. Sprinkle bell peppers, onion, beans, and zucchini with cumin and oregano, and toss in the remaining oil. Spread vegetables in one layer on a large baking sheet and bake on lower rack of oven, turning frequently, for 15 to 20 minutes or until tender and browned.
4. Transfer cooled scallions to blender and puree with lime juice, vinegar, and mustard. With motor running, add broth in a slow, steady stream. Season with salt and pepper and set aside.
5. Separate radicchio leaves, rinse and dry. Tear leaves into pieces and toss with enough scallion mixture to lightly coat. Arrange warm roasted vegetables over the radicchio and pass remaining scallion vinaigrette separately.

SERVES 4

APPROXIMATELY 1.7 GRAMS FAT PER SERVING

◆ ◆ ◆ ◆ ◆

EGGPLANT AND
TOMATO CASSEROLE

▶ ▶

M y rendition of this classic is slimmed down in fat but
still rambunctious with flavor. Enjoy it as an antipasto,
side dish, or light meal for four with just a small salad, or
serve it as a first course followed by grilled or roasted
poultry.

2   *large eggplants (about 2¹/₂ pounds)*
    Vegetable oil cooking spray
3   *large cloves garlic, chopped*
1   *28-ounce can no-salt-added plum tomatoes,*
    drained and chopped
1   *tablespoon red wine vinegar*
¹/₄ *cup coarsely chopped mixed basil and parsley*
    leaves
1   *teaspoon dried thyme*
    Salt and freshly ground pepper to taste
¹/₂ *cup low fat shredded Swiss cheese*

1. Peel eggplants, cut into ¹/₂-inch-thick rounds, and set
aside.
2. Coat a deep nonstick skillet with cooking spray and
sauté garlic over medium-low heat until softened. Raise heat
to medium, add tomatoes, vinegar, and herbs, and cook for
15 minutes, stirring occasionally. Taste and add salt and pepper, if desired.
3. Preheat broiler.
4. Arrange eggplant on a baking sheet lightly sprayed

with cooking oil and broil, turning once, for about 15 minutes or until lightly browned on both sides. Remove baking sheet from oven and adjust oven temperature to 350°F.

5. Spoon a thin layer of tomato mixture into an ovenproof casserole, cover with a layer of eggplant and a sprinkle of cheese. Repeat until all ingredients are used, ending with cheese. Cover and bake for 15 minutes, then remove lid and bake for an additional 10 minutes or until lightly browned and bubbly.

SERVES 8 AS A SIDE DISH
APPROXIMATELY 2.2 GRAMS FAT PER SERVING

◆ ◆ ◆ ◆ ◆

WILTED SPINACH
WITH TANGY SAUCE

▶ ▶

I like sesame seeds a lot, but because of their high oil content, I use them sparingly, as in this dish where their nutty, slightly sweet flavor makes them almost invaluable.

For optimum results, toast the sesame seeds in a clean, dry skillet, shaking the pan constantly until they begin to color slightly or a few start to pop. Then, when the spinach is ready, combine it with the dressing in a serving bowl, toss gently and garnish with the sesame seeds. Serve warm, at room temperature, or chilled.

    1½   *pounds fresh spinach, trimmed and well rinsed*
     1   *tablespoon sesame oil*
     1   *teaspoon sugar, or to taste*
     2   *tablespoons red wine vinegar*
    1½   *tablespoons low sodium soy sauce*
     1   *teaspoon prepared Dijon mustard*
     1   *tablespoon toasted sesame seeds*

1. Cut spinach into large pieces and steam in only the water clinging to the leaves just until wilted. Refresh immediately in cold water, drain, and gently squeeze out as much moisture as possible.

2. Whisk together sesame oil, sugar, vinegar, soy sauce, and mustard, toss with spinach, and serve sprinkled with sesame seeds.

SERVES 4
APPROXIMATELY 4.5 GRAMS FAT PER SERVING

◆ ◆ ◆ ◆ ◆

RED POTATO SALAD DIJON

▶ ▶

I must confess to a terrible weakness for potato salads. You know the kind I mean, the ones prepared the old-fashioned way (*loaded with mayonnaise*). This is a wonderful recipe that allows me to eat my fill without the least worry about seriously hiking up my fat gram count for the day.

1	tablespoon balsamic vinegar
1	tablespoon cider vinegar
1	teaspoon prepared Dijon mustard
1	tablespoon light mayonnaise
1/4	cup low fat plain yogurt
1	large stalk celery, diced
1	small red onion, diced
3	tablespoons boiling water
1 1/2	pounds small red potatoes in skin, boiled,
	drained, cooled to lukewarm (*do not refrigerate*)
	Salt and freshly ground pepper to taste
2	tablespoons chopped fresh chives

1. In a small bowl, combine vinegars with mustard, mayonnaise, and yogurt. Let stand for at least 15 minutes to blend flavors.

2. In large bowl, combine celery and onion and pour boiling water over. Let stand for about 10 minutes. Meanwhile, slice cooled potatoes.

3. Add vinegar mixture to onion mixture and blend

well. Add potatoes and toss to coat. Season to taste with salt and pepper. Transfer to a serving bowl and sprinkle with chives.

SERVES 4
APPROXIMATELY 2.0 GRAMS FAT PER SERVING

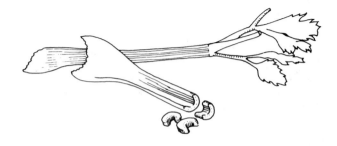

DESSERTS

◆ ◆ ◆ ◆ ◆

BANANA BUTTERMILK ICE CREAM

▶ ▶

Loaded with potassium, calcium, and vitamins A, B, and C, it's no wonder bananas have been called the world's perfect food. Happily, bananas are available year round—as are the rest of the ingredients called for in this dessert. Top with fresh banana slices before serving, if desired.

2   cups evaporated skim milk, chilled
1   cup ripe, mashed banana (about 2 small)
1   cup low fat buttermilk
$^1/_2$ cup sugar
$1^1/_2$ teaspoons light brown sugar
2   tablespoons half-and-half

1. Combine all ingredients in the bowl of a food processor and process until smooth.

2. Transfer mixture to ice cream maker and freeze according to manufacturer's instructions. (If you do not have an ice cream maker, pour mixture into shallow trays and freeze for about 2 hours or until slushy. Chop up and spoon into bowl of food processor, process until creamy, and return to freezer until about half frozen. Repeat process twice more, then spoon into a container and freeze solid. Transfer to refrigerator for about 15 minutes before serving to soften slightly.)

MAKES ABOUT 4$^1/_2$ CUPS
APPROXIMATELY 1.0 FAT GRAM PER $^1/_2$ CUP

CAPPUCCINO CREAM SHERBET
(Adapted from Margaret Sullivan)

► ►

This full-flavored sherbet looks particularly inviting when served in frosty champagne or any other long-stemmed glasses and makes a grand finale to an elegant dinner. Great with thin vanilla wafers or just on its own.

1	packet unflavored gelatin
1/4	cup cold water
1 1/2	cups freshly brewed hot espresso or strong coffee
1/2	cup evaporated low fat milk
1/4	cup half-and-half
1/4	cup sugar
1/2	teaspoon vanilla extract
1/8	teaspoon ground cinnamon

1. In the bowl of a food processor, sprinkle gelatin over cold water and let stand for 2 minutes. Pour in coffee and process with a few on/off motions to dissolve gelatin.

2. Add remaining ingredients and process until well blended. Chill mixture until very cold, transfer to ice cream maker and process according to manufacturer's instructions. (If you do not have an ice cream maker, pour mixture into a shallow tray or baking pan and freeze for about 2 hours or until mushy. Chop up and spoon into bowl of food processor and process until smooth. Return to freezer until nearly frozen, and whip again. Repeat process once more, then transfer to covered container and freeze until solid. Transfer container

to refrigerator for about 15 minutes before serving to soften slightly.)

MAKES ABOUT 3½ CUPS
APPROXIMATELY 1.1 GRAMS FAT PER ½ CUP SERVING

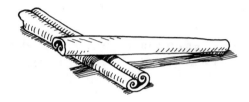

◆ ◆ ◆ ◆ ◆

LIGHT-AS-AIR
CHOCOLATE SOUFFLÉS

▶ ▶

Soufflés are those cloudlike mixtures made with a thick egg yolk–based sauce or puree that is lightened by folding in stiffly beaten egg whites. Dessert soufflés may be baked, chilled, or frozen and are usually flavored with purees of fruit, liqueurs, or with chocolate as in the recipe below.

Low in fat per portion even with the whole egg used here, the cocoa will provide the chocolate taste we all crave without the obscenely high butterfat content of block chocolate.

Although soufflés must be prepared immediately before baking and served as they come out of the oven, I find that enlisting the aid of a friend to serve the main course gives me the time I need to get them ready.

> *Vegetable oil cooking spray*
> 2 *tablespoons plus ¼ cup sugar*
> ¼ *cup evaporated skim milk*
> 1 *teaspoon vanilla extract*
> 1 *large egg yolk*
> ¼ *cup unsweetened cocoa*
> 6 *large egg whites, at room temperature*
> ½ *teaspoon cream of tartar*

1. Preheat oven to 375°F. Coat eight ½-cup soufflé cups with cooking spray, sprinkle with 1 tablespoon sugar, and set aside.

---

2. Heat evaporated skim milk with vanilla extract in a small saucepan until hot but not boiling. Beat egg yolk and 1 tablespoon sugar until creamy. Whisk a small amount of hot milk into egg mixture, then lift saucepan off heat and incorporate egg mixture back into saucepan. Add cocoa and stir over very low heat until completely blended. Remove from heat and set aside.

3. In a large, grease-free bowl, beat egg whites until foamy, sprinkle in cream of tartar, and beat until soft peaks form. Sprinkle in remaining ¼ cup sugar gradually and beat until stiff, glossy peaks form. Pour chocolate mixture carefully down the side of the bowl and fold into beaten egg whites.

4. Divide mixture among prepared soufflé cups and set on a large baking sheet. Bake in preheated oven for 15 minutes or until well puffed and cracking on top. Serve immediately.

SERVES 8
APPROXIMATELY 1.7 GRAMS FAT PER SERVING

◆ ◆ ◆ ◆

PEACH MELBA PIE

▶ ▶

Peach Melba, the fabulous dessert created by fabled French chef Escoffier to honor opera star Nellie Melba, is classically made with syrup-poached peaches, rich vanilla ice cream, and raspberry sauce.

Loving the flavors but wanting something different (and less fattening), I created this pie using local peaches and the last raspberry harvest of the year. It's the perfect ending to a cool late summer's eve supper.

1	cup unbleached all-purpose flour
¹/₄	cup whole wheat pastry flour
¹/₄	cup rolled oats
¹/₄	teaspoon salt
1	tablespoon vegetable oil
¹/₄	cup evaporated skim milk
¹/₄	cup thawed frozen apple juice concentrate, approximately
	Vegetable oil cooking spray
3	cups peeled, sliced fresh peaches (about 6 medium), tossed with 2 tablespoons fresh lemon juice
¹/₂	teaspoon vanilla extract
¹/₄	teaspoon ground nutmeg
¹/₄	teaspoon ground coriander
¹/₄	cup plus 2 tablespoons sugar, approximately
2	cups fresh raspberries, picked over and rinsed
3	tablespoons quick cooking tapioca, divided in half

1. Combine flours, rolled oats, and salt in a medium bowl. Add oil, milk, and juice concentrate and mix with two forks until moist and crumbly. If necessary, add additional juice a teaspoonful at a time. Shape into a ball, wrap in plastic, and chill for 30 minutes. Try not to handle the dough any more than is absolutely necessary or it may toughen.

2. Coat a 9-inch pie pan lightly with cooking spray (do not use a glass pie plate or the edge of the crust will brown too quickly). Roll out dough and fit into pie pan, trimming and reserving any extra dough. Roll reserved dough scraps lightly into a ball, cover in plastic wrap, and return to refrigerator.

3. In a medium bowl, combine peaches and any accumulated juices, vanilla extract, spices, and ¼ cup sugar. Set aside. In a small bowl, toss raspberries with remaining 2 tablespoons sugar and set aside for about 15 minutes.

4. Preheat oven to 475°F.

5. Prick bottom and sides of crust in pie pan with a fork. Spoon raspberry mixture onto crust and sprinkle with 1½ tablespoons of the tapioca. Spoon peach mixture on top and sprinkle with remaining tapioca.

6. Remove reserved dough from refrigerator, unwrap and roll out thinly. Cut out decorative shapes and arrange on top of fruit mixture. Sprinkle with 1 teaspoon sugar, if desired.

7. Bake for 10 minutes on center rack, then immediately reduce heat to 425°F. and bake for an additional 30 minutes or until crust is brown and filling is bubbly. Remove to rack. Serve lukewarm or at room temperature.

SERVES 8

APPROXIMATELY 3.0 GRAMS FAT PER SERVING

♦♦♦♦♦

VANILLA CUSTARD
IN CARAMEL SAUCE

▶▶▶▶▶▶▶▶▶▶▶▶▶▶▶▶▶▶▶▶▶▶▶▶

This creamy dessert made with evaporated low fat milk has a tiny fraction of the fat of the traditional custard recipe.

Timing the cooking is difficult, but starting with a preheated oven and a boiling water "bath" surrounding the custard cups helps.

> ¹/₄ *cup plus 3 tablespoons sugar*
> 4 *teaspoons water*
> 2 *large eggs*
> ²/₃ *cup whole milk*
> 1 *12-ounce can evaporated low fat milk*
> 2 *teaspoons vanilla extract*

1. Preheat oven to 300°F.

2. Mix ¼ cup sugar with water in a small, heavy saucepan and cook over medium-low heat until sugar is dissolved. Increase heat, cover pan and bring to a boil, swirling the pot frequently. When it boils, remove the lid and let mixture boil, continuing to swirl the pot and watching the mixture carefully, until it begins to color. When it is just golden, remove it from the heat immediately and divide the caramel among the bottoms of six ½-cup custard cups, swirling it as well as you can to coat the bottoms of the cups. The mixture will harden fairly quickly. Set prepared cups aside.

3. Set a kettle of water on the stove to boil. In a medium bowl, combine eggs with remaining 3 tablespoons sugar,

---

stirring gently but thoroughly. When blended, gradually add the whole milk, evaporated low fat milk, and extract. Whip mixture gently to avoid creating bubbles.

4. Divide custard among the prepared cups and set the cups in a large baking dish. Pour boiling water into the dish to come about halfway up the sides of the cups, and immediately set the baking pan in the center of the preheated oven. Bake for about 1 hour and 15 minutes or until set.

5. Remove from oven and cool at room temperature, then refrigerate and chill completely. Can be prepared one day ahead and refrigerated, covered well with plastic wrap.

6. To serve, run a sharp knife carefully around the rim of the cup, cover cup with a dessert plate, invert, and custard and sauce should slide out.

SERVES 6

APPROXIMATELY 3.6 GRAMS FAT PER SERVING

♦ ♦ ♦ ♦ ♦

CHOCOLATE STRAWBERRY "CREAM" PIE

▶ ▶

I f you thought there was no place for cream pie in your low fat life-style, you're in for a tasty surprise!

Although this luscious pie should be assembled only a few hours before serving, the crust can be prepared in advance and refrigerated.

1¹/₃	cups chocolate wafer crumbs (about 25 wafers)
1¹/₂	tablespoons margarine or butter/margarine blend, melted
1	tablespoon cooled prepared coffee, approximately
¹/₄	cup cold water
1	packet unflavored gelatin
2¹/₂	cups sliced fresh strawberries plus 6 large whole strawberries for garnish
1	teaspoon fresh lemon juice
¹/₂	cup plus 2 tablespoons sugar
¹/₂	cup evaporated skim milk, chilled in bowl in freezer for 45 minutes (chill beaters as well)
1	teaspoon vanilla extract
4	large egg whites, at room temperature
¹/₄	teaspoon cream of tartar

1. Preheat oven to 350°F.

2. Combine chocolate wafer crumbs with margarine until crumbs are coated as well as possible, then drizzle in coffee to make a coarse but moist mixture. If mixture seems dry, add more coffee by the ¹/₂ teaspoonful.

---

3. Press mixture evenly onto the bottom and up the sides of a 9-inch pie plate. Bake for 10 minutes, remove from oven, and cool completely on a rack. (Can be made ahead and refrigerated, well wrapped, for 24 hours).

4. Combine water and gelatin in the top bowl of a double boiler and let stand for 3 minutes.

5. While gelatin mixture sits, chop sliced strawberries and lemon juice in a food processor until nearly pureed, then transfer mixture to a medium bowl and stir in $1/2$ cup sugar.

6. Heat water in double boiler and stir gelatin mixture until dissolved. Remove from heat and let cool just slightly. Fold gelatin mixture into strawberries and chill for about 30 minutes or until mixture begins to thicken but is not set.

7. When strawberry mixture is just about chilled, remove bowl, beaters, and evaporated skim milk from freezer (there should be a large rim of slush in the bowl) and beat with vanilla extract until nearly tripled in volume. Refrigerate briefly.

8. In a grease-free bowl, whip egg whites over low speed until frothy, add cream of tartar and beat until soft peaks form. Sprinkle in 2 tablespoons sugar and beat until peaks are stiff and glossy.

9. Remove strawberry mixture from refrigerator, top with whipped milk and then beaten egg whites and gently but quickly fold milk and egg whites into strawberries.

10. Pour mixture into prepared crust and chill until firm.

11. Rinse reserved whole strawberries and slice thin from bottom point up toward stem, leaving stem end just barely intact. Spread slices into a fan shape, place 4 equally spaced around rim of pie and 2 in center.

SERVES 8

APPROXIMATELY 5.1 GRAMS FAT PER SERVING

◆ ◆ ◆ ◆ ◆

FROZEN LEMON SURPRISE

▶ ▶

M ake this splendid dessert in plenty of time to let it chill properly. Don't be afraid to experiment with other citrus fruits and flavor combinations.

6   *large lemons*
1   *cup sugar*
4   *cups low fat plain yogurt*
1   *teaspoon vanilla extract*
2   *fresh tangerines, peeled and sectioned or 8-ounce can, packed in juice*
    Mint leaves for garnish

1. Cut 1 inch of top off lemons and set tops aside. With a grapefruit spoon or melon baller and working over a bowl, scoop out lemon pulp. Scoop any pulp out of tops as well. Strain pulp and reserve juice (you should have about ½ cup juice; if not, juice an additional lemon to make up the difference). Cut enough peel off of the bottom of the lemon just so that it will sit upright without cutting completely through the shell. Set shells aside.

2. Pour ½ cup of the sugar onto a shallow plate. Dip lemon shells in cold water just about up to the cut tops, taking care not to immerse them, pat them with a paper towel so they remain barely moist, then roll quickly in sugar. As each shell is well coated with sugar, place it upright in a shallow glass baking dish. Coat all shells and then tops, replace tops, and immediately place baking dish in the freezer.

3. Combine lemon juice, yogurt, remaining ½ cup

sugar, and vanilla extract and blend well. Transfer mixture to a shallow pan and place in the freezer. When partially frozen (about 2 hours), remove from freezer and whip until creamy.

4. Remove lemon shells from freezer, lay 2 tangerine sections in the bottom of each shell, divide yogurt mixture evenly among shells, replace tops and return shells to freezer. Freeze solid. Transfer to refrigerator for 20 minutes before serving to soften slightly.

SERVES 6

APPROXIMATELY 2.6 GRAMS FAT PER SERVING

◆ ◆ ◆ ◆ ◆

LIGHT TART CRUST

▶ ▶

This basic recipe yields a light, crispy tart crust suitable for a wide variety of desserts requiring a pastry crust. Tarts may be filled with any number of fresh fruits—your choices are a matter of seasonal and market availability and personal taste.

The apple juice concentrate used in the recipe is a suggestion only. Feel free to substitute any other fruit juice concentrate or sweetener.

$^2/_3$ cup unbleached all-purpose flour
$^1/_4$ cup rolled oats
$^1/_4$ teaspoon salt
$1^1/_2$ tablespoons margarine or margarine/butter blend, melted
4 tablespoons thawed frozen apple juice concentrate, approximately, heated
Vegetable oil cooking spray

1. In the work bowl of a food processor, combine flour, oats, and salt. Process with a few on/off motions just to blend.

2. With machine running, add margarine and process briefly (mixture should be very crumbly and dry), then add apple juice concentrate in a thin stream until mixture begins to form a ball. You may need slightly less or more than 4 tablespoons. Wrap ball in plastic wrap and chill for 30 minutes (may be made 24 hours ahead).

3. Preheat oven to 375°F. Spray a 10-inch tart pan lightly with cooking spray and set aside.

---

4. Lay a large piece of waxed paper or plastic wrap on a dampened surface and lay ball in the center. Flatten it with the heel of your hand and then roll from the center outward (use a lightly floured rolling pin) into a 12-inch-diameter circle. It will be quite thin.

5. If possible, roll the crust back onto the rolling pin and unroll it over the prepared tart pan. If paper comes up with the dough, stop rolling, invert tart pan over crust and turn pan upright with waxed paper, then gently peel paper off. Lightly press crust into pan.

6. Prick dough several times with a fork and bake for 15 minutes or until just beginning to turn golden. Cool and fill.

MAKES ONE 10-INCH TART CRUST (8 SERVINGS)
APPROXIMATELY 18.8 GRAMS FAT PER WHOLE CRUST

◆ ◆ ◆ ◆ ◆

CUSTARD FRUIT TART

▶ ▶

Imagine! Fresh seasonal fruit set in a yogurt-based vanilla cream resting on a bed of apricot jam spread on a crisp tart base. . . .

Before presentation, lightly score four times across the diameter to assure eight equal portions, and decorate with mint leaves.

    1   packet unflavored gelatin
    ¹/₄ cup cold water
    2   cups (16-ounce container) low fat vanilla yogurt
    1   Light Tart Crust (page 200), baked and cooled
    ¹/₄ cup no-sugar-added apricot fruit spread
    3   cups fresh fruit (such as blueberries, sliced straw-
        berries, raspberries, green or red seedless grapes,
        sliced kiwifruit)
        Mint leaves for garnish

1. Combine gelatin with water and let stand 3 minutes, then heat mixture in the top of a double boiler or set over a bowl of very hot water and stir until gelatin is dissolved.

2. Combine gelatin mixture with yogurt and chill for 15 to 30 minutes or until thickened but not completely set.

3. Spread prepared crust with apricot fruit spread, spoon on prepared yogurt cream and chill for 30 to 45 minutes or until pastry cream is set. Top with desired fruit and chill until serving time. Garnish with mint leaves, if desired.

SERVES 8
APPROXIMATELY 4.0 GRAMS FAT PER SERVING

♦ ♦ ♦ ♦ ♦

PINEAPPLE SNACK CAKE

▶ ▶

This attractive, golden pineapple cake is relatively simple to prepare and extremely low in fat.

	Vegetable oil cooking spray
1½	cups cake flour plus extra for dusting pan
1	large egg
¼	cup sugar
2	tablespoons light brown sugar
1½	teaspoons baking powder
¼	teaspoon each: ground ginger, nutmeg, cinnamon, allspice, and cloves
½	teaspoon salt
1	8-ounce can unsweetened pineapple rings in juice
	Confectioners' sugar

1. Preheat oven to 350°F. Lightly coat an 8-inch-round cake pan with cooking spray, dust with flour, and set aside.

2. In a medium bowl, beat egg with sugar and brown sugar until creamy.

3. In a small bowl, sift together 1½ cups flour, baking powder, spices, salt, and pineapple juice from the can (you should have about 6 tablespoons of juice) and stir into the egg mixture until well blended.

4. Cut pineapple rings into chunks and fold into batter. Pour or spoon batter into prepared pan and bake for about 40 minutes or until golden and springy to the touch.

5. Remove from oven and cool 15 minutes on a rack.

Dust with confectioners' sugar and serve slightly warm or at room temperature.

SERVES 6
APPROXIMATELY 1.0 GRAM FAT PER SERVING

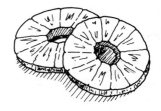

APPLE PEAR SHORTCAKES WITH GINGER CREAM
(Adapted from Penelope Nichols)

▶ ▶

This dessert may have strayed far from the traditional, but the combination of juicy, gently spiced apples and pears provides an admirable alternative. It is guaranteed to satisfy any craving for shortcake whether strawberries are in season or not.

The cakes and fruit filling can be prepared in advance, but whipped evaporated milk will eventually lose volume, so prepare the topping shortly before serving.

2	cups sifted cake flour
1	tablespoon baking powder
$^1/_2$	teaspoon salt
1	tablespoon light brown sugar
$^1/_2$	teaspoon ground coriander
4	teaspoons diet margarine
$^1/_2$	cup skim milk, approximately
2	large, ripe pears, peeled, cored, and sliced
2	tart medium apples, peeled, cored, and sliced
$^1/_2$	cup water
1	tablespoon thawed frozen apple juice concentrate
$2^1/_2$	tablespoons sugar
1	cup evaporated skim milk, chilled in bowl in freezer for 1 hour (chill beaters as well)
$^3/_4$	teaspoon powdered ginger

1. Preheat oven to 450°F.

2. In a large bowl, resift flour with baking powder, salt, brown sugar, and coriander. Cut in margarine until mixture is crumbly (this can be done in a food processor, using quick on/off motions). Add ½ cup skim milk and work into dough lightly. If dough is too dry, add additional skim milk 1 tablespoon (and only a trace of fat) at a time until dough is silky but not sticky.

3. Turn dough out onto a board and knead 4 or 5 times. Dough should be worked as little as possible. Roll or flatten to a thickness of about ½ inch and cut out or shape into eight 3½-inch rounds.

4. Place dough rounds slightly apart on an ungreased baking sheet and bake for 15 minutes or until lightly golden.

5. Meanwhile, combine pear and apple slices with water and cook over medium heat until fruit is tender and liquid is evaporated by about ¾. Lower heat, add apple juice concentrate and 1½ tablespoons sugar and cook until liquid is syrupy. Remove from heat and cover.

6. Remove evaporated milk from freezer (it should have a large rim of slush around the edges), add ginger and remaining tablespoon sugar and whip until light and creamy. Split shortcakes in half, top the bottoms with fruit and syrup and a portion of cream, and replace tops. Drizzle with a little remaining syrup and serve at room temperature.

SERVES 8
APPROXIMATELY 1.6 GRAMS FAT PER SERVING

INDEX